# WHERE YOU FIND GOD

*By the same author*

MEN OF FIRE
WOMEN OF LIGHT
SEE YOURSELF IN THE BIBLE

# WALTER RUSSELL BOWIE

## *Where You Find*

# GOD

HARPER & ROW, PUBLISHERS

*New York, Evanston, and London*

FIRST EDITION

LIBRARY OF CONGRESS CATALOG CARD NUMBER: 68-11727

L-R

To
BETTYE BURKE
flawless secretary
and encouraging friend

# Contents

# WHERE YOU FIND GOD

# I

## The Necessary Choice

FIFTEEN hundred years ago the man named Augustine—who probably had not the faintest notion that he would eventually be called St. Augustine—wrote his *Confessions,* which have been handed down in manuscripts and then printed and reprinted from that time to this. The important thing about him was that he expressed the fact which every human being sooner or later has to recognize: namely, that a man has two sides to himself, and somehow he has got to deal with both. Augustine first was a man-of-the-world, in the full sense of that term. He was content with the man-of-the-world's adjustment to things as they happened to be, without requiring of himself any longer purposes or any more disciplined behavior than the average. At least he was content with that most of the time—as men in every generation may seem to be. But the trouble was that there was something else he could not get rid of. Another side of his nature kept telling him that there was a mightier fact which he had managed to forget. What if there was God, and a will of God for him that would not let him go? With part of himself he wanted to follow his own easy impulses, which

1

had been "strengthened by long indulgence." But he could not follow that self-will with complete abandonment. "These two wills, one old one new, one carnal the other spiritual, contended with each other and disturbed my soul."

Now it is true that as one looks about on life one may not see at any particular moment conspicuous instances of that sort of disturbance. Many of us are going along casually without asking any fundamental questions. The routine of everyday affairs seems to take care of itself. As long as things go smoothly, there seems no need for anything we do not have—or which, if we do not have, we may hope to get tomorrow. Look at the advertisements in the magazines. Alluring pictures of what the new house may be made to look like, the new model car, the color television, foods and wines; *Newsweek, Life,* the sports page and the financial reports in the morning paper—aren't these enough to satisfy immediate interest? Sometimes it can seem so. In this twentieth century which appeared so smoothly promising, numberless people tended to think that there would be no problems big enough to be very bothersome. Everybody could get ahead if he wanted to. Graduate from school or college, pick up a good job, get married, settle down in suburbia, make money, be a part of the untroubled crowd that says to itself, "We have it made."

But what keeps that from being the whole picture? Two facts.

One is the discovery that material advantage cannot be nailed down as surely as self-confidence may have assumed. Now and then there are tremors in the ground. The big financial opportunity which was promised does not materialize, the expected promotion falls through, the leadership in politics or in community affairs—and the prestige that belongs to it—goes to somebody else. We read in the *Rubáiyát:*

The worldly Hope men set their Hearts upon
Turns Ashes—or it prospers; and anon
  Like Snow upon the Desert's dusty Face
Lighting a little hour or two—is gone.

And the second fact is a man's discovery—or a woman's
equally—that even if things can be manipulated outside,
this may not mean that life can be managed inside. To get
what we have wanted does not guarantee that it will bring
joy when we have got it. The business or profession which at
first looked so exciting may sink into a drab routine. The
dream house which cost so much to build may not turn out
to be the kind of home to which one comes back with happiness at the end of the day. Love may have gone sour,
between husband and wife, between parents and children.
Underneath the surface of an affluent existence, with its glit-
ter and excitement, there are dark currents of anxiety. For
life to be hectic may not mean that it is happy. With more
than any people in history have ever had to live on, more
and more of us, both the old and the young, are beginning to
ask, "What are we living *for*?"

Not long ago it seemed natural, and altogether to be expected, that the younger generation should be optimistic.
"Even if those who have had their way with things have
made a bad business of it all, the rising forces will do better.
There's solid ground to build on, and wherever there is confi-
dence great achievements can be built." That is how nearly
everybody said it was and would be at the beginning of the
century when it appeared that our new proud tower could
be made to reach up—though the tower of Babel could
not—to the sky. "But just when we are safest, there's a
sunset-touch."[1] Two world wars, the Korean war, Vietnam;
more young men drafted, more killed—and less assurance as
to what all the killing could accomplish. Many in their inner
apprehension have echoed the title of the book which Paul

[1] Robert Browning, "Bishop Blougram's Apology," from *Men and Women.*

Tillich wrote and launched on its wide reading, *The Shaking of the Foundations*. With the splitting of the atom and the development of the hydrogen bomb, a dark cloud of dread lies along the horizon. Only recently it was assumed that in this earth of ours "a place was provided in which life could grow and history develop, in which words could be heard and love be felt, and in which truth could be discovered and the Eternal adored." But science has given to man the power to annihilate himself and his world. And some of the scientists who have brought about that triumph, awed by the immensities which they have unleashed, "are speaking today, like the true prophets of the past . . . not of progress, but of a return to the chaos of the beginning; not of peace, but of disruption; and not of happiness, but of doom."[2]

If those words should be literally true then there would be no use of talking any more. If our stupidities and our savageries have brought us to the point of human obliteration, then we are dealing with something worse than a conflict between two wills, which Augustine said disturbed his soul. He believed there was a will of God which man could be grasped by, and that this will meant to be redemptive, and *would* be redemptive if man yielded himself to God's infinite compassion and his saving grace. But what if man has got past saving? Or what if it is naïve now to believe any more in a God real enough to save?

*Then* what?

---

[2] *The Shaking of the Foundations* (New York: Charles Scribner's Sons, 1948), pp. 3, 5.

# II

## God in the Intensity of Life

"GOD is dead."

That is the pronouncement which has been put forth in this decade by a group of radical thinkers, and this in further words is what it means: "That there once was a God to whom adoration, praise and trust were appropriate, possible, and even necessary, but that now there is no such God."[1]

It is no wonder that such a declaration waked a startled attention like an alarm bell sounding in the night. The reaction to it has included of course those who make instant response to any new sensation; newspapers and periodicals, "columnists" who must be ready with quick opinions, commuters on the morning trains and subways who see the headlines and tell the nearest fellow passengers what they ought to think. Some who have religious associations and move generally in conventional circles will declare that any talk about "God is dead" is nothing but an outrage. What will happen to respectable society if that sort of idea gets going? Such are the various ways in which conversation might run in many quarters.

[1] Thomas J. J. Altizer and William Hamilton, *Radical Theology and the Death of God* (Indianapolis: Bobbs-Merrill, 1966), p. x.

But as a matter of fact and in plain honesty, how much difference would it make to the general run of people if a conviction of God did begin to disappear? Some difference, no doubt; but reaching how deep? There would be a jolt to familiar ideas, and everybody resents that kind of unexpected disturbance. The assumed fact of God up there somewhere is part of the accepted order of things. It is like the frame and glass protecting a picture in the house that men and women have looked at ever since they were children and is part of the family associations. Break the frame and take down the picture and there is a blank space on the wall; and nobody likes that, because the empty spot keeps being a reminder that something accustomed is gone. It was and is more comfortable to note that God's name is linked with the pledge of allegiance to the flag, that "In God we trust" is stamped on the money everybody uses, and that if we seem to be—and why not?—the favored people of the earth, it must be because this is properly "God's country." Even ordinary speech may appear to have a sort of religiousness in it when people swear by the name of God once in a while. Consequently, there was a clamor when the Supreme Court ruled that prayer and Bible reading might not be an official part of the regimen in the public schools. But the fact that the supposedly pious demand for some sort of recognition of God may have to do more with form than with substance was set forth in one of the thrusting cartoons of Herblock, when he drew a picture of a man and his wife and two school-age children at the breakfast table. The father is indignantly holding up the morning paper with headlines of the Supreme Court decision, and blurting out: "What do they think? That we have got to listen to the kids saying their prayers here at home?"

So it is true that the resentment some people express when they hear it said that "God is dead" is only sound and fury —and mostly sound. For them God has not yet been movingly alive. They are not the ones chiefly to be concerned about lest the present ferment in religious thinking should be destructive. They have not possessed what has substance enough to be capable of destruction. What needs to be hoped concerning them is that the present-day discussions, even if such discussions may sometimes seem unconventional and rude, may wake some vital thinking about God in those who have never really thought—or cared much— about God before.

But there are others about whom there can be real concern in these days when so much that is said and written brings disturbance to what, for many, had been a simple faith. These are the men and women whose conceptions of God have been very limited, but who have had a genuine devotion to what they thought God was, and to what they thought he wanted them to be and do. They have carried along with them the best that they learned from their mothers, or from someone else in whose eyes they saw a light that came from something higher than this earth. From human love they had got a feeling that beyond the human love which held them there was a larger love that they could trust. So they believed in God, with a child's instinctive manner of believing. They knew there were many questions about him which they could not get answered when they asked them, so they just accepted that fact and went on believing anyway that he was there. Their pictures of God were not far from the naïve and lovely simplicity of *Green Pastures*, that dramatic symbol of plantation Negroes' faith, in which God in a human form both homely and majestic looked down upon his earth with troubled compassion, seeing his children's willfulness and wrongs, yearning to make them good, and wondering whether there was anything left to do except to answer the urging of Gabriel "to pass a miracle."

*That* picture of God, of course, cannot live any more in

our sophisticated world which has moved out of the realm of imagination that belongs to the child or to a childlike people. But what shall we put in its place? Here is where the trouble comes for great numbers of men and women who have grown up with religious assumptions. They know now that the forms of thought in which their belief in God once seemed secure are broken. The universe of modern knowledge has grown so gigantic and so perplexing that the conceptions of God which were so simple and instinctive for the small boy and girl must change to something greater. We cannot see God any more as on a throne up there in the sky, taking charge of everything—not when the sky itself has dissolved into the awful immensities of the endless interstellar space. We cannot echo what Robert Browning made the flower girl Pippa sing, "God's in his heaven; all's right with the world"—not when it looks sometimes as though the world were about to turn into a crazy welter of blind impulses and savage confusion. Most people who have been brought up religiously are not going to swallow the raw assertion that "God is dead." But they do get vastly troubled when they try to find some answer to their wondering as to what he may be and where he may be found. They know that they feel adrift and lonely, with a loneliness like that of the Breton fisherman aware that "the sea is so great, and my boat is so small."

The extraordinary number of books about religious faith or nonfaith which have been written lately, and the astonishing circulation of some of them, testify to a hunger which is latent in most human minds and hearts: the hunger to discover an ultimate Reality which will give some coherent sense to what they think and do. Granted, as we have already recognized, that many people seem to float along on the surface of existence, without asking any deeper questions. Yet these also have their moments when they are jolted into a more imperative concern. The urge to be honest with himself may come some time to every man. The one who has had little or no belief may wake to the fact that he does need something to believe in. And the person who has supposed that he already had a religious faith that was sufficient may discover that it was built on foundations which are sinking under him—the foundations of immature ideas which he had never examined but which he has got to dig down to and look at now. Earlier in this century disturbing signs made plain that the old and beautiful cathedral at Winchester in England was in imminent danger of collapse. The piles driven into the ground on which the walls had rested had disintegrated, and there was acute necessity to fill in with stone and concrete where the ancient piles had been. That is what has to be done, as the years go by, with the structure of religious convictions in a human being. Forms of thought which belonged to other centuries must be replaced or undergirded by the strength of newer certainties; and that is what a book like *Honest to God* was meant to help contemporary people begin to do.

Let it be recognized that even the most challenging and disturbing questions about the accepted form and content of religious beliefs need to be listened to with a steady regard for what new truth they may contain. These questions—and even what seem to be denials—have not come from "loud mockers in the roaring street," but from men who have held responsible posts as teachers in the churches. A deeply perceptive theologian[2] who does not share the negative emphases of these new spokesmen has seen that, even in their negations, "a most astonishing thing in the premises—there is no despair" but evident hope; and he quotes what William Hamilton has written in *Radical Theology and the Death of God*.

We try out new words, we pray to God to return, and we seem to be willing to descend into the darkness of unfaith and doubt that something may emerge on the other side. . . .

[2] Clifford L. Stanley, *Conflicting Reports about God* (Washington, D.C.: Lectern Press, 1967), p. 4.

Our waiting for God, our godlessness, is partly a search for a language and a style by which we might be enabled to stand before him once again, delighting in his presence.

There can be a thoughtful willingness not only among those who might be at the fringes of the Christian fellowship, but also among those who stand near the center of it, to consider in this present time new ways of thinking and of speaking. "I am convinced," wrote John A. T. Robinson, Bishop of Woolwich, "that there is a growing gulf between some of the traditional conceptions of God in which our faith has been framed and the categories which the 'lay' world (for want of a better term) finds meaningful today." There must be "a radical recasting," he thinks, of the structure of Christian belief "in the process of which the most fundamental categories of our theology—of God, of the supernatural, and of religion itself—must go into the melting. I can at least understand what those mean who urge that we should do well to give up using the word 'God' for a generation, so impregnated has it become with a way of thinking we may have to discard if the Gospel is to signify anything."[3]

That, to be sure, would seem a rather drastic prescription to have to take through the period of what it is hoped might be our religious convalescence. But suppose we did adopt it. Suppose we put a moratorium on the use of the term "God" because notions so nearly infantile have entered into what many have thought that God is and does. What more up-to-date word or set of words can we find which will serve our thinking better?

There is "the Ground of Being." That is the term which Paul Tillich, one of the most influential thinkers of the mid-twentieth century, has made familiar. He would help us to realize that God is not to be looked for as separated from ourselves, not "up there" or "out there," but as that which

---

[3] *Honest to God* (Philadelphia: Westminster Press, 1963), pp. 7-8.

undergirds all that we experience everyday. Those who analyze the human mind and spirit have developed, as he has pointed out, "the so-called 'psychology of depth.' It leads us from the surface of our self-knowledge into levels where things are recorded which we knew nothing about on the surface of our consciousness. It shows us traits of character which contradict everything that we believed we knew about ourselves. It can help us to find the way into our depth, although it cannot help us in an ultimate way, because it cannot guide us to the deepest ground of our being and of all being, the depth of life itself."

Then Dr. Tillich went on:

The name of this infinite and inexhaustible depth and ground of all being is *God*. That depth is what the word *God* means. And if that word has not much meaning for you, translate it, and speak of the depths of your life, of the source of your being, of your ultimate concern, of what you take seriously without any reservation. Perhaps in order to do so, you must forget everything traditional that you have learned about God, perhaps even that word itself. For if you know that God means depth, you know much about Him. . . . You cannot think or say: Life has no depth! Life itself is shallow. Being itself is surface only. If you could say this in complete seriousness, you would be an atheist; but otherwise you are not. He who knows about depth knows about God.[4]

We may not grasp at once the full substance of those words, but we can move in the direction to which they point. Every one of us knows that he does not exist all by himself. Now and then we feel that we are part of something so great and so significant that no ordinary words can express the fullness of it. It may be on some morning when you are up early and see the sun rise, and breathe the first freshness of the breaking day; or when your little child looks up at you; or when you start off to work and are glad that you belong in

[4] *The Shaking of the Foundations* (New York: Charles Scribner's Sons, 1953), pp. 56-57.

a human group that has something worthwhile to do and strength with which to do it. Then also your consciousness may go deeper. One day you ask yourself, "In the midst of these experiences, who and what am I? What does my life *mean?* And what is it that I really care most about?" When you have reached down to the level of that questioning, you may not talk about a "Ground of Being," but you may have a new and reverent sense of the dimensions of existence, and a feeling of something *there* in this life of ours which no casual self-sufficiency would have known.

The way ahead out of the religious perplexities of these times will not depend upon our definitions. It may start from what Anne Morrow Lindbergh has called "immersion in life." That is the title of an account she has written of a safari without guns in Africa, a going out into the open to look and listen and try to become absorbed for a little while into another world of consciousness. By day and night she drew close to the creatures of the wild; impala, zebra, giraffes; rhinoceros and buffalo; lions emerging from the bush, and herds of elephants at the water holes. She writes:

For a brief period one seems to escape the limits of one's own species, the prison bounds of the human body, as if one had shed a skin and become another creature with other senses and powers. . . . One listens, as primitive man once listened, in mystery and apprehension. . . . One stands in sober wonder before this tidal wave of life, overwhelmed by its power. . . . And in the act of looking, something of a creative act takes place—a leap of imagination. One goes half way to participation in the life of other creatures, feels oneself a part of their actions. Something inside oneself leaps as they leap, or is quiet beside their cropping quiet, or watches with their alert watchfulness. One is stilled in their stillness, a stillness trembling with life like the stillness of a flame. And in this moment of participation, one has made the connection—or rather is suddenly aware of it. The act of imagination is an act of obeisance to life in another creature—life in an unfamiliar yet related form. And by this act of imagination, and by every act of imagination, one is enriched. For the act of obeisance to life, wherever one makes it, is in essence religious.[5]

It is striking to note that in this account of inner experience which comes to its climax in the words "in essence religious," there is no mention of the name of God. Here would seem to be implicit reinforcement to the assumption of Bishop Robinson that "we should do well to give up using the word 'God' for a generation, so impregnated has it become with a way of thinking we may have to discard"—a way of thinking, he means, which associates God with occasional miraculous acts rather than with the mystery and wonder of the realities we encounter every day. A brief and vivid book entitled *The Real God*, by Alfred B. Starratt, has sought to show where there can be a directly open door between a modern scientific understanding of our universe and a new awareness of the spiritual meaning to be discovered there.

"It is urgent," he writes,

that someone should make an attempt at expressing the relationship between modern physics and modern religion, for until we are able to do so we shall continue to be saddled with what Bertrand Russell called "Sunday truths." For an hour on Sunday morning churchgoers talk and act as if God were a kind of glorified human being who lives somewhere above the blue sky. During all the other hours of the week they know this isn't so. . . . We have become men of conflicting allegiance. Our loyalty to our religious heritage and our loyalty to the demonstrated power of scientific knowledge work needlessly against each other. To reintegrate our divided will, we need an integrated view of reality.

Once it was held by all men that the universe is made up of two kinds of ultimate stuff. One of these was called matter, the other energy. . . . But one of the greatest scientific minds in all history, Albert Einstein, showed that this picture is false. He saw that there is one ultimate reality because matter and energy are

[5] *Life,* October 21, 1966.

variant forms of the same thing. . . . Matter is energy. Energy is matter. The explosion of the first atom bomb demonstrated that the distinction between the two is only one of a temporary state. . . . The one ocean of energy is a flowing, changing, dynamic reality which is continually shaping itself into new forms of existence. . . . Einstein's construct . . . has replaced the construct of the universe drawn by Isaac Newton which explained the universe as a gigantic machine. Men concerned with ultimate reality cannot ignore the difference that this new understanding makes in religion as well as in other fields of human interest and action.[6]

Yes, this new understanding of the universe does make a difference: the difference first of all of conceiving creation not as something complete, but immediate and continuous; not as something finished back there in seven days described in the first chapter of the Book of Genesis, but as going on increasingly now.

All well and good thus far, it might be conceded. But the ordinary human heart is not going to be satisfied with an impersonal energy or with a "Ground of Being," stated in those terms. If there is a God we can be glad of, a God whom we can really worship, and not a God who—no matter how philosophically correct he may sound—just leaves us cold, then he will have to be something less chilly and abstract than a Ground of Being. How can I imagine the Ground of Being to have any concern for me, or to consider that it makes any difference what I or any other of us poor humans feel toward it? How can any prayer I might address to what sounds so remote bring any kindling of mind and heart such as generations of men and women have known when they said, "Our Father"?

There are some forms of words in our current theological writings which we listen to with polite respect, but which simply do not bring us what we long to have. The best we

[6] *The Real God* (Philadelphia: Westminster Press, 1965), pp. 15, 16, 18.

could say of them is like what a little girl wrote to her grandmother who had given her a pincushion for Christmas: "Thank you so much for making it for me. I always did want a pincushion—but not very much."

What we are reaching out for is to find a God who is the *Heart* of Being. We need some sense that God is not merely something that has produced us, as the ground produces grain—and also weeds; but that he is the pulsebeat of all life, and that the warmth of his life flows into us and is at every moment the strength by which we live. To speak the word "heart" is to be brought near to the thought of that which loves; and when all is said and done, no conception of God will mean much to us unless we believe that somehow the Being that is back of our little existence cares. Francis Thompson, in the great poem for which his name is best known, wrote of the infinite Reality which follows us with "deliberate speed, majestic instancy," and he used the startling simile of "The Hound of Heaven." But what had seemed to be the Hound is revealed at last as the Love that will not let us go.

If then there is indeed a living Spirit which is reaching out toward us, the way to know that it *is* there must be by what Anne Morrow Lindbergh called "immersion in life." She felt the mystery and wonder of the life that undergirds all existence as she drew close to the "inexhaustible vigor" of the creatures of the wild. But if the fullness of the reality that may be in God is to be apprehended, "immersion in life" must have to do also with our highest human contacts. Only as we are living at the full scope of our own personalities in a world of persons can we come into vital touch with God if God himself is all that we mean—and more than what our imperfect words can mean—by personal. Neo-orthodox theology led thought for a while up a blind alley when it talked of God as the Wholly Other, "the unheard-of, unrecognized, mysterious person, who cannot be discovered anywhere in the world."[7] On the contrary, it is when we go out most fully into life and see the little glimmerings of infinity which may be in human souls that we grow conscious of the one supreme Self of whom our partial selves are fragments that bear witness to him who is the whole. The trouble with us is that so often we are shut up within our egocentricity, little frozen units of self-concern. Then we are so small that it is impossible to have any great belief. But when we reach out beyond ourselves, something great can happen. A man begins to be concerned for other people. His friendships expand, and all his generous interests widen. Life has dimensions now that it did not have before. And if one day he falls in love, then it has dimensions beyond what he had ever glimpsed. He finds his self entering into, and being entered by, another self. He becomes aware that his own existence becomes meaningful only as he is developing those creative sympathies through which he shares something above and beyond this common earth with other souls. There is much that he cannot put into words, and much about theology which he cannot explain, but deep down in himself he knows that he is finding God.

It is this openness to life that alone makes possible the communication to us of the living realities which are beyond ourselves and yet can enter into us. I could assume, if I chose, that all that I look out upon is nothing more substantial than a shadow-show, that there are no persons solidly existing except myself—or at any rate, none worth my being concerned about. I could ignore them or rebuff them, and so they could never come close to me or enrich my grudging personality by what their comradeship was ready to give. We can act in the same way toward that which might be God. "There is no proof of God," a man may say, "in any

[7] Emil Brunner, *The Theology of Crisis* (New York: Charles Scribner's Sons, 1929), p. 33.

books I read; and until I do have proof, I am not going to be a dupe of religious credulity." So he may shut himself up in what has been called "snarling logicality," and block the roads by which all the while God might be coming through.

This fact that the reality of God, if it is to be experienced, must be found not through speculations and arguments but through immersion in life, shines out in one of the startlingly vivid events recorded in the Old Testament—an event all the more vivid because it emerges out of what seemed at first complete perplexity. Moses in the wilderness, having fled for his life from Egypt, sees a vision of "a flame of fire out of the midst of a bush; and he looked, and lo, the bush was burning, yet it was not consumed"(Exodus 3:2); and then he heard a voice that bade him go back to Egypt and lead his people of Israel out of Egyptian bondage into freedom. Before that moment, any such commission might have seemed to Moses inconceivable. He had killed an Egyptian taskmaster, and therefore to go back where Pharaoh's wrath could reach him would be at mortal peril. It appeared as though any worthwhile possibility for his life was finished. But there was the bush that burned with fire, "yet was not consumed." And this is what it meant: the awareness deep down in Moses' soul of something stronger than himself, the flame of conscience and unfinished duty, burning, burning, refusing to sink down into ashes, holding him accountable to a will for his life that would not let him go. So he heard the voice that was for him the voice of God commanding him to go back to Egypt. And then what? Then he began, as every human being might, to express his doubt and hesitation; and most fundamentally his uncertainty about whether he really knew anything and could say anything about God. Suppose the people of Israel should ask him what he knew about God. What should he say then? Would God please tell him what to answer, tell him who God is and what is his name?

Then came the reply which for the moment must have seemed to Moses only a blank. The voice said to him, "I Am Who I Am"; or as another translation of the Hebrew has it, "I Will Be What I Will Be." What sense could Moses make of that? In the first sound of the baffling words, nothing. But out of what seemed only an enigma, the great disclosure could arise. God would become manifest to Moses not while he lingered in the wilderness, but only when he returned to Egypt and dared the unmeasured risk of leading the people of Israel in the exodus. It was as though the divine Reality had said to Moses, "You cannot know me by any words that could be spoken; not by any definition, or by any fleeting signs. Who and what God is must be revealed in the life experience of the man who reaches out to God. God is the whole profound meaning of life that is and that is to be, as this meaning gradually and continually is set forth. You will know me only as day is added to day, and from every day lived in loyalty to the highest you then know, you gather your increasing understanding of what life and God can mean."

This same living fact was what William James was reflecting when he wrote *The Will to Believe*. Of course he did not mean that a man should determine blindly and irrationally to believe in God—or tell himself that he believed— simply because he wanted to. But what he did mean was that it is stupid to conclude that God is dead because somebody has come along and tied crêpe to the door of a religious formulation which God was supposed to inhabit; and stupid also to suppose that faith must be carried out to its funeral because some professor in a philosophical classroom asserts that his abstract arguments demonstrate that no one with academic respectability can believe that faith is still alive. "When I look at the religious question as it really puts itself to concrete men," wrote William James, "and when I think of all the possibilities which both practically and theoretically it involves, then this command that we shall put a stopper on our heart, instincts and courage, and *wait*—acting of course meanwhile more or less as if religion were *not* true—till doomsday, or till such time as our intellect and senses working together may have raked in evidence enough —this command, I say, seems to me the queerest idol ever manufactured in the philosophic cave."[8] In other words, get up and go out to the challenge of life and duty—as Moses did—following the faith that God may reveal himself *there,* and see what happens.

When one reads the history of great human souls who have made this venture and notes the power that came to them—Elijah, Amos, Paul the apostle, Martin Luther, John Wesley and others too many for their names to be written down—it would seem at least that God has been a long time dying; and as one looks about, one may see that the power has not vanished now. A man whose spoken and written words are listened to by many hundreds every week has said this: "I know that when I am helpless and feel that the things I have to do I cannot do, there is Someone greater than I who helps me. In ways I cannot predict and sometimes do not recognize the help comes."[9]

And in the autobiography of Harry Emerson Fosdick, *The Living of These Days,* there is a reference to "a youth conquered by alcohol and in utter despair," who found a help beyond himself which he had not known existed. To the general public, Dr. Fosdick was chiefly known as the great preacher who stood alone each Sunday in the pulpit of the Riverside Church; but one of the supreme aspects of his ministry was the intimate help he gave to troubled individuals who flocked to him for personal counseling. Said this particular youth, "I don't believe in God, but if *you* do, for

[8] New York: Longmans, Green & Co., 1898, p. 29.
[9] Theodore P. Ferris, *What Jesus Did* (New York: Oxford University Press, 1963), p. 104.

God's sake pray for me, for I need him!" "That was a challenge to everything I believed and preached," wrote Fosdick. "Few experiences . . . had so deep an effect on me as the battle in which that youth and I for long months engaged."

It ended in victory; and this was the final witness to it: "If you ever find anyone who does not believe in God," the youth said at last, "send him to me. I know."[10]

# III

## *The Presence Back of History*

EXPERIENCE can outweigh argument. A kindling thought
that comes to us as though out of the blue, an inner urge
toward some new faithfulness, a deep assurance in time of
stress that "there is someone greater than I who helps me"—
these are experiences which have made human souls believe
in the reality of God. The whole Bible is full of that conviction; and through many generations men and women who
have grown up familiar with the Bible have felt the inspiration of it for themselves. In this part of their awareness they
are not likely to listen much to those who tell them that God
is dead. There is a fact for life as to which they can say, like
the young person mentioned in the preceding chapter who
talked with Dr. Fosdick, "I know."

But the religious faith which has come down through
Judaism and Christianity goes beyond the affairs of individuals. It proclaims a God who moves in the great events of
history.

Have you not known? Have you not heard?
  Has it not been told you from the beginning?

Have you not understood from the foundations of the earth?
It is he who sits above the circle of the earth,
    and its inhabitants are like grasshoppers;
who stretches out the heavens like a curtain,
    and spreads them like a tent to dwell in;
who brings princes to nought,
    and makes the rulers of the earth as nothing.

Isaiah 40:21-23

That is a sublime assertion. But to the unbeliever it may seem to be mere rhetoric; magnificent rhetoric, if you choose, but only rhetoric as distinguished from reality. The idea of a transcendent power who affects the events of earth is rejected by many who consider themselves to belong to a more enlightened age. One of the Russian cosmonauts who first orbited this planet and cruised in outer space, made the jaunty comment that he saw no sign of God. There was no one sitting on a heavenly throne "above the circle of the earth."

Also there can be more specific challenge to what has seemed to be biblical belief. Only a warped idea of history could result—say some of the contemporary disputants—when men were naïve enough to think that a God up in heaven was guiding it, and would guide it according to their special desires if they urged him enough. Back of the Old Testament was the plain belief that Israel had a particular relationship with a sovereign God, and that consequently everything would turn out the way they wanted it. Look at the Book of Psalms, for example, and see some of the promises which men considered to have been divinely given, and therefore could be relied on.

Ask of me, and I will make the nations your heritage,
    and the ends of the earth your possession.
You shall break them with a rod of iron,
    and dash them to pieces like a potter's vessel.

Psalm 2:8-9

Transgressors shall be altogether destroyed.

Psalm 37:38

Did it actually happen that way in biblical times? the challengers ask. Does it ever happen thus conveniently to be a fact that there is a God in heaven who reaches down to advance the interests of those who worship him? What was there as a matter of fact in the history of "the Chosen People" to indicate that the God they trusted was *there* in their time of need? They might have expected conspicuous deliverance in their times of danger; but much of the time what they got was directly the reverse. Their country was repeatedly overrun, Jerusalem destroyed, thousands carried away into captivity. So the trust they wanted to have in a living God might have seemed only an illusion. Right from the Bible itself there come voices that express the near-eclipse into which faith could fall.

> Thou hast made us the taunt to our neighbors
> the derision and scorn of those about us
> Thou hast made us a byword among the nations,
> a laughing stock among the peoples.

Psalm 44:13-14

> O Lord, how long shall I cry for help,
> and thou wilt not hear?
> Or cry to thee "Violence!"
> and thou wilt not save?

Habakkuk 1:2

Some of the "new theologians" consider those cries of doubt and disillusionment to be the inevitable final word. Their conclusion can be "That there is no God and that there never has been."[1] In regard to the whole Bible story, Paul van Buren has written:

---

[1] William Hamilton in Altizer and Hamilton, *Radical Theology and the Death of God* (Indianapolis: Bobbs-Merrill, 1966), p. x.

The mythological view of the world has gone, and with it the possibility of speaking seriously of a *Heilgeschichte,* a historical drama of salvation, in which God is said to have acted at a certain time in the world to change the state of human affairs.[2]

Granted that there has been the emergence of some creative good. Still it is argued that this has come only from human beings who were developing a little more mature intelligence and morality within themselves, and not from any influence larger than the unpredictable accidents of this earth.

Moreover it can be maintained that the kind of supernatural belief which seems to be embodied in the Old Testament can be not only illusory; it can be definitely hurtful. What may happen when men suppose they can call on an almighty power to advance their interests? They may try to use their religion as a sanction for their own ambitions, and an outlet for some of the fiercest passions of the human heart. This is what one may hear in the psalms as one who prides himself upon his own pious status contemplates his enemy:

> May his days be few; may another seize his goods!
> May his children be fatherless, and his wife a widow!
> May his children wander about and beg.
> May they be driven out of the ruins they inhabit!
>
> Psalm 109:8-10

And as for the enemies of the whole people of Israel, especially the Babylonians:

> Happy shall he be who takes your little ones
> and dashes them against the rock!
>
> Psalm 137:9

> The posterity of the wicked shall be cut off.
>
> Psalm 37:38

[2] *Ibid.,* p. 32.

. . . that you may bathe your feet in blood,
    that the tongues of your dogs
    may have their portion from the foe.

                                        Psalm 68:23

So it might be made to appear that much of what the
Bible witnesses to has been discredited.

But the ultimate reckoning is not so quickly made. All the
facts need to be looked at with courageous honesty, to see
whether there is the central truth of a living God which like
the anvil can wear out many hammers.

In the first place, there should be sifted out the conceptions which are *not* central. The reality of God is not to be
equated with the distorted thoughts which men have sometimes had of him, nor with the twisted desires which they
wanted him to serve. The imprecatory psalms and other ut-
terances like them reflect a God who is dead and ought to be
dead—and never was alive except in unredeemed imagination. What has died is not God but the idols of pride and
passion which men have sometimes put in his place. The
most radical critics of conventional religion deserve not any
attempted rebuttal but unqualified thanks when they have
shown some of the perversions which men who thought they
were religious have been led into. When the Jews in the
times of the Old Testament, or men and women of the Christian era right down to this present year, have assumed that
God must be at their disposal to satisfy their personal emotions, including their ferocities, they have reduced the infinite holiness to a kind of private Moloch to whom their
enemies could be brought for sacrifice; and it is no wonder
then that there are those who say, "Let's hear no more of
God."

In the second place, it must be recognized that much of
the biblical portrayal of the ways in which the living God
was believed to have been manifest has got to pass through
radical rethinking. The heart of the agelong Judeo-Christian

faith has been that an eternal Reality higher than all our small vagaries did enter in and does enter in to shape our destinies, and that history is more than a random interaction of human forces and a meaningless confusion of good and evil. Daring to believe that, and interpreting each stage of history in the light of it, the people of Israel expressed what they believed by picture and projections; and our necessity is to see *through* these to the central faith which life must test.

As happenings were told of and retold, the instincts which are always present in human tradition led to enlarged recital of the original events. Patriotic emotions glamorized what a cool objectivity would have described in soberer terms, and literal facts grew into dramatic legends. When the people of Israel were trying to gain entrance into Canaan, Joshua on a certain day won a victory so surprising that it was accounted as a miracle, and to the later chronicler it seemed that God himself must have prolonged that day so that Joshua's victory could be complete. Consequently it was written that Joshua had said:

> "Sun, stand thou still at Gibeon,
> and thou Moon in the valley of Ajalon."
> And the sun stood still, and the moon stood
> until the nation took vengeance on their enemies.
>
> Joshua 10:12-13

Likewise, in the much more crucial event of the exodus from Egypt, the deliverance of Israel under the leadership of Moses is put into a supernatural framework. The Israelites trying to escape by night from Pharaoh came to water which they had to cross. Biblical scholarship suggests that this was the relatively shallow "Sea of Reeds" or "Papyrus Lake," which could have been passable at the moment Moses seized, when a strong east wind blew; but would not have been passable for Pharaoh's chariots when the wind had changed. For the people of Israel and for all their subsequent history, the fact of their escape was of such transcendent importance that no ordinary description of its manner could seem sufficient to represent what happened. Accordingly there grew the tradition that the passage had been through the wide and formidable Red Sea, and made possible by a visible intervention of the power of God which enabled the Israelites to pass through the Red Sea "on dry ground," with the waters being "a wall to them on their right hand and on their left" (Exodus 14:22). Similarly again and again in the Old Testament narratives there appear conceptions of God almost as mythological as the conceptions elsewhere of the gods of Olympus. God may be heard "walking in the garden in the cool of the day" (Genesis 3:8). God says, "Come, let us go down" to see what men were up to when they tried to build the tower of Babel, and to scatter them over the face of the earth (Genesis 11:7). And according to the prophet Samuel, God commanded Saul, the king of Israel, "Now go and smite Amalek, and utterly destroy all that they have; do not spare them, but kill both man and woman, infant and suckling, ox and sheep, camel and ass" (I Samuel 15:3) Therefore it is not strange that when this sort of thought of God is crudely passed on in the human mind we can have Hollywood spectaculars presenting a God who appears as the convenient worker of theatrical marvels; or in some smug books supposed to be religious, as "The Man Upstairs."

A growth in knowledge and a better understanding of the ascending levels of thinking in the Bible have long since made sensitive people know that the reality of God and his ways of working are not the same as the kindergarten pictures which even in the Bible have been drawn of him. Some of the pictures can be laid aside; but all the while there stands the massive fact that some extraordinary influence did make the history of Israel different from that of other

nations. It was not in vain that the psalmists declared: "In
thee our fathers trusted; they trusted, and thou didst deliver
them. . . . In thee they trusted, and were not disappointed"
(Psalm 22:4-5). Through the whole Old Testament and
going beyond it, there has been the faith that there is "a
power *not ourselves* that makes for righteousness," and that
in the long run this faith stands vindicated. No one can pin-
point any era of history and demonstrate that here or there,
in this crisis or in that, indisputably it was God who turned
the scales. Our short perspectives cannot prove the dated
presence of One with whom "a day is as a thousand years,
and a thousand years as one day." There were times of darkness and near-despair when it seemed to the people of Israel
that the God in whom they had trusted was not there. But
the actuality is that Israel has endured through the long
centuries while vast forces that threatened it have vanished
from the earth. The monuments of Assyria show in their
stone bas-reliefs the bearded warriors and the iron chariots
of an empire that seemed indestructible—one of whose com-
manders, according to the Book of Isaiah, could fling this
taunt to the defenders of besieged Jerusalem: "Has any of
the gods of the nations delivered his land out of the hand of
the king of Assyria? Where are the gods of Hamath and
Arpad? Where are the gods of Sephavaim? . . . Who among
all the gods of these countries have delivered their countries
out of my hand that the Lord should deliver Jerusalem?"
(Isaiah 36:18-20). Nevertheless, Jerusalem as a city was to
stand until after Assyria had gone down to destruction; and
Jerusalem as a symbol of spiritual ideals that move the
hearts of men outlasts time.

Babylon, the magnificent, could have its day of dominion,
and King Nebuchadnezzar might well have walked "on the
roof of the royal palace" and exclaimed, "Is not this great
Babylon which I have built by my mighty power as a royal
residence and for the glory of my majesty" (Daniel 4:29-30).

But Babylon today is only a dust-heap in the desert, and out of it has come no influence that endures.

"Ah, yes," may come the reasonable answer. "Assyria vanished, and Babylon was destroyed; that is true. But so also was it true of those who called themselves the children of Abraham. As a nation, aspiring to material power, they also sank into insignificance. What corporate greatness did they have? And the people as human individuals, with their poignant hopes and fears—what deliverance came to them? Look at what the Jews have suffered through the many centuries. Remember Hitler and the Nazi Storm Troops and the extermination camps. How can it be said that the history of Israel has been any *Heilgeschichte*, and what evidence does it furnish that there ever is in human history anything but indiscriminate fate?"

Who can confront that question without having thought and feeling stretched to the breaking point? No finite mind can fathom the problem of evil, and the contradictions in history which it presents. One moves into what seems the darkness, and gains only a broken understanding of what the mystery is that must be grappled with. Why, in a world that was meant for goodness, has wickedness often been so strong? Perhaps the most that we can recognize is that if men were to be responsible beings and not robots they had to have the awful freedom to rebel against the holy purpose that created them; and, because of that rebellion, then in the clash of human events the innocent would be bound to suffer. Their suffering, like the suffering of the servant in the prophecy of Isaiah, may be redeeming; and for those who are part of the vicarious sacrifice, one dares to trust that our little perspective opens out into an eternal one, and that "the souls of the righteous are in the hands of God."

Meanwhile, beyond our sins and blunderings and their tragic cost, life and human destiny may be guided in channels deeper than we can see; not in the cross-currents that have to do with kings and kingdoms and prestige and power and the towers of Babel of our pride, but with preparing the ground out of which the characters of men may grow. The patient wisdom which our fretfulness can seldom recognize may be disclosed at length in what at the moment appeared only as disaster. In the sixth century B.C., when Jerusalem was captured by the Babylonians and all the hopes of the Jewish people seemingly were shattered, the prophet Jeremiah saw a redeeming will which in the end would be more significant than any short-range reckoning could appraise. Out of material reverses a people might gain eternal values. "Behold, the days are coming, says the Lord, when I will make a new covenant with the house of Israel and the house of Judah. . . . I will put my law within them, and I will write it upon their hearts, and I will be their God, and they shall be my people" (Jeremiah 31:31, 33). The ultimate God who molds men's destinies is not "a cozy God who is content to be met in a garden or on a golf-course." Human life must include "exaltations and agonies, in which also God is known." And God must "be met, as Jacob met him in the Genesis story, in wrestling; in and beyond tragedy."[3] Thus the supreme meaning of history, and the element in it which can be recognized as divine, is the letting loose in the world of men of long-range creative forces more important than any immediate events.

That such creative forces *were* let loose is the reason why some of the great periods recorded in the Bible can be accounted as "sacred" history.

Authoritative modern scholarship attributes the essential content of the Ten Commandments to Moses, that heroic figure who was inspired to lead the exodus from Egypt. The account of the way in which the Commandments were transmitted, as written in the Book of Exodus, is set in a

---

[3] David L. Edwards, in *The Honest to God Debate* (Philadelphia: Westminster Press, 1963), p. 43.

framework of mystery and awe; the legendary framework of God descending upon Mount Sinai amid "thunders and lightnings and a thick cloud," while "the people were afraid and trembled and stood afar off " . . . as "Moses drew near to the thick cloud where God was" (Exodus 19). Thus what came to be recognized as the immense meaning of the Commandments was symbolized in this picture of a *mysterium tremendum;* but more important than the symbolism is the actual substance of what happened there at Sinai. For in the Ten Commandments there was stamped upon the mind of the Jewish people, and through them transmitted to the world at large, the conviction that all real worship of God must be expressed not in ritual but in the conduct of life.

"What then do you chiefly learn from the Ten Commandments?" asks the Office of Instruction in the Book of Common Prayer; and the answer is: "I learn two things from these Commandments; my duty towards God and my duty towards my neighbor." That is what generations of the human race for more than three thousand years *have* learned —or have had the chance to learn—from the Commandments: the need of loyalty to a sovereign Righteousness, and of integrity in all human relationships because of what that Righteousness enjoins. They have been rightly called the Magna Charta of the social order, and "a supreme factor in the agelong process of kneading decency into the human race."[4]

Some four centuries after Moses there appeared the formidable figure of the prophet Elijah. He confronted Ahab, king of Israel, as Ahab moved toward the gate of the vineyard of Naboth which the royal power had evilly seized. In one of the great first instances in history of championship of the common man, Elijah denounced the king with a flaming

[4] J. Edgar Park, in *The Interpreter's Bible* (Nashville: Abingdon Press, 1952), Vol. I, p. 980.

indignation that made Ahab cringe. What made him formidable? Not any force which he himself possessed. Rather, his assurance that there exists an invincible moral authority which men cannot ultimately defy, so that he could dare to say, "Thus saith the Lord!"

After Elijah came the other prophets: Amos, with his terrible indictment of social wrongs and his cry, "Let justice roll down like waters, and righteousness like an ever-flowing stream" (5:24); Hosea, declaring in God's name, "I desired mercy and not sacrifice, and the knowledge of God more than burnt offerings" (6:6); Isaiah, bringing the message which had come to him in the temple from "The Lord, high and lifted up":

> cease to do evil,
>     learn to do good;
> seek justice,
>     correct oppression;
> defend the fatherless
>     plead for the widow.
>
> Isaiah 1:16-17

Else, though men might make many prayers, God would not listen, for—

> Your hands are full of blood.
>
> Isaiah 1:15

Were Moses and Elijah and Amos and Isaiah and Jeremiah only transient voices speaking nothing more profound than the ideas they happened humanly to hold? Or through them was it the Infinite that was speaking?

If there is indeed a mighty purpose that moves through human history and gives it meaning, it would be presumptuous for any finite human mind to think that it could fully see that meaning and at any single moment interpret it aright. Yet there are times when through what might have seemed to be only the collision and contradiction of mortal events there sounds a vaster note. Within the moral consciousness a bell is set to ringing—not by its own motion, but caught up in the reverberations of a bell of judgment deeper than its own. So it may have been with the seers and prophets of bygone centuries who saw eternal forces moving in the shifting scenes of time—and so it may be with those in any century perceptive enough to see the silent rivers that run beneath the surface of events which is all that most men see. Victor Hugo, in *Les Miserables*, wrote of Waterloo:

Was it possible that Napoleon should have won that battle? We answer No. Why? Because of Wellington? Because of Blücher? No. Because of God.

Napoleon had been denounced in the infinite, and his fall had been decided on.

He embarrassed God.[5]

What Victor Hugo wrote was only one expression of the conviction that rises up again and again in the moral consciousness of mankind—that there is a sovereign Righteousness, and that unbridled self-assertion must reckon with a final power against which no defiance can prevail. Herbert Butterfield, Professor of Modern History in Cambridge University, has similarly written: "There seems to be one fundamental law of a very solemn kind. . . . Judgment in history falls heaviest on those who come to think themselves gods, who fly in the face of providence and history, who put their trust in man-made systems and worship the work of their own hands."[6] And Reinhold Niebuhr, in the 1930's, began a lecture with these words: "It is often asked, 'Does the state belong to God or to the devil?' And the answer is: 'The state belongs to God; but it is in danger of becoming the devil by imagining that it is God.' "

The agelong Judeo-Christian faith has been and is that this earth, with the human life upon it, was created not for

[5] "Cosette," Book I, chap. 9.
[6] *Christianity and History* (London: Fontana Books, 1957), p. 82.

brutishness, but rather that it might move forward to the largeness of spirit and the generous imagination which shall make men become at length the family of the children of God. If that be true, and if that is the meaning and sign of God in history, then it was something more than the balance of earthly forces that brought about the fall of insatiate empires such as those of Assyria and Babylon, and frustrated "The Invincible Armada" of Philip of Spain. Adolf Hitler, invoking again the pagan gods of violence, poured contempt on "peaceful competition of nations" and set out to work his unhindered will. In his name it was proclaimed, "Germans! Never forget that you are a member of the master race!"[7] Therefore Germany, told by Dr. Robert Ley, head of the Nazi party machine and of German labor, "tough, brawling, hard-drinking," that "the Führer is always right,"[8] launched under Hitler's leadership upon its demonic course of attempted world dominion. But Adolf Hitler, who boasted that his Third Reich would last for a thousand years, ended in the ashes of his Berlin bunker. There was a power in the moral universe more invincible than he.

To believe that an influence more than mortal may operate in history, it is not necessary to suppose that such an influence in order to be real must manifest itself in miracles. The eternal Spirit can work its will through the power of spirit: through awakening in great human individuals, and through them at length in the masses of men, the integrity of motive, the flaming purpose, and the unflagging courage, by which the decisive weight is thrown into the scales for righteousness. This power coming from the Unseen may appear to the earthly minded to have no existence, but actually it may be the divine dimension in relation to which all history must be read. As one of the most incisive thinkers of this

---

[7] William M. Shirer, *Berlin Diary* (New York: Alfred A. Knopf, 1941), p. 513.
[8] *Ibid.*, pp. 590, 270.

century has written in *The Varieties of Religious Experience:*

The further limits of our being plunge, it seems to me, into an altogether other dimension of existence from the sensible and merely "understandable" world. Name it the mystical region, or the supernatural region, whichever you choose. So far as our ideal impulses originate in this region (and most of them do originate in it, for we find them possessing us in a way for which we cannot articulately account), we belong to it in a more intimate sense than that in which we belong to the visible world, for we belong in the most intimate sense wherever our ideals belong. Yet the unseen region in question is not merely ideal, for it produces effects in this world. When we commune with it, work is actually done upon our finite personality, for we are turned into new men, and consequences in the way of conduct follow in the natural world upon our regenerative change. But that which produces effects within another reality must be termed a reality itself. . . . I only translate into schematic language what I may call the instinctive belief of mankind: that God is real since he produces real effects.[9]

It is a perilous thing to think that God is dead. The Nazis of Germany thought so. The Communist regimes of Russia and China may think so now. The result is that a nation may become so obsessed with its hard ambitions, and so wrapped up in its imagined self-sufficiency, that it grows contemptuous of any ultimate accounting. It assumes that there is no effective moral truth before which it must stand for final judgment, and that instead it can pursue and win its own advantage, no matter at what outrage to what may once have been the conscience of mankind. Meanwhile, it would be a hidden folly which could lead to tragedy for any nation which boasts a Christian heritage, including ours, to think that therefore it will not fall under judgment. It is possible always for a people whose intentions are good to become

[9] William James (New York: Longmans, Green & Co., 1903), pp. 515-517.

possessed by "the arrogance of power," to lose the capacity for self-criticism, and to assume in its imagined rectitude that it is appointed to play God to lesser peoples of the earth. Not only from ancient facts, but from the solemn portents of the future, may sound the truth of the psalmist's words:

> Thou dost deliver a humble people;
> but the haughty eyes thou dost bring down.
>
> Psalm 18:27

# IV

## Can Life Really Be "Religionless"?

IN the world of religious thought—and rethinking—one of the most significant persons of the mid-twentieth century was Dietrich Bonhoeffer, the young German pastor and teacher imprisoned by the Nazis for nearly two years, and then executed in April, 1945. William Hamilton, in *Radical Theology and the Death of God*,[1] ranks Bonhoeffer as "the most decisive theological influence on the younger generation of Protestants today." It is Bonhoeffer also who seems to have captured the thought of Bishop John A. T. Robinson and stirred the impulse which led to the writing of *Honest to God*. "I must register," he says, "the impact of the now famous passages about Christianity 'without religion' in Dietrich Bonhoeffer's *Letters and Papers from Prison*. I first encountered extracts from these in . . . January 1952. One felt at once that the Church was not yet ready for what Bonhoeffer was giving us as his last will and testament before he was hanged by the S.S. Indeed, it might be understood properly only a hundred years hence. But it seemed one of those trickles that must one day split rocks. . . . I knew

[1] Indianapolis: Bobbs-Merrill, 1966.

that this was something we must learn to assimilate."[2]

Bonhoeffer endured the long months of his imprisonment, and what might have been the shattering impact of its loneliness, with magnificent steadfastness and courage. Caught in a situation and in a time when evil seemed triumphant, it was for him as though the centuries had turned back and Christianity stood again in the age of the catacombs and the martyrs. He could have understood—as those whose convenience and complacency can never understand—the awful depths of the cry upon the cross, "My God, my God, why hast thou forsaken me?" Nevertheless, he held to a faith which not only sustained himself, but brought inspiration to others who came in contact with him. In one of the last weeks before his execution, when he had been removed from his Berlin prison to Buchenwald and then to Flossenbürg, a captured British officer who saw him there and was later rescued and set free by the Allied armies when Nazi Germany collapsed, wrote of him, "He always seemed to diffuse an atmosphere of happiness, of joy in every smallest event in life, and of deep gratitude for the mere fact that he was alive. . . . He was one of the very few men that I have ever met to whom his God was real and close to him."[3]

But it was this same Dietrich Bonhoeffer who in some of his last letters expressed thoughts concerning God which have shaken accustomed conceptions, and have seemed to Bishop Robinson "one of those trickles which must one day split rocks."

What is it that he was saying; and in what ways have there come from him, on the one hand, an inescapable challenge to a kind of Christianity which seems unrelated to the present world, and on the other hand—and much more commanding and important—an ultimate evidence of the God to whom his life bore witness?

[2] Philadelphia: Westminster Press, 1963, pp. 22-23.
[3] *Prisoner for God, Letters and Papers from Prison* (New York: The Macmillan Co., 1954), p. 11.

First, his challenge to conventional and complacent religion. It had no limited reference, as will abundantly grow clear; but it comes into sharpest focus as one remembers the facts in Germany, and especially in Nazi Germany, which Bonhoeffer had to confront. In the Lutheran Church there was a long tradition of separation between what was assumed to be sacred and what was looked upon as only secular. Religion was the cultivation of individualistic piety, and not a concern for the things of earth. God must be found in the church; the state and government and political decisions belonged to a sphere of their own. Consequently great numbers of the pastors of the German church, and the people following their lead, made terms with Hitler. They would go to church and say their prayers and seek their own salvation, and meanwhile consider it part of the natural order of things that Hitler should be the Führer for whatever had to be decided outside.

Bonhoeffer rejected that dichotomy of life. From the early 1930's he was involved in the resistance movement. It was because of this that he was arrested and finally put to death. He saw that a man of conscience would not find God but lose him if he thought that God must be looked for only somewhere else than in the desperate realities of men's secular existence.

From his prison he wrote:

During these years the church has fought for self-preservation as though it were an end in itself, and has thereby lost its chance to speak a word of reconciliation to mankind and the world at large. So our traditional language must perforce become powerless and remain silent, and our Christianity today will be confined to praying for and doing right by our fellow men. Christian thinking, speaking and organization must be reborn out of this praying and this action. . . . It is not for us to prophesy the day, but the day will come when men will be called again to utter the word of God with such power as will change and renew the world. It will be a new language, which will horrify men, and yet overwhelm them by its power. It will be the language of a new righteousness and truth, a language which proclaims the peace of God with men and the advent of his kingdom.[4]

And again.

The Bible does not recognize our distinction of outer and inner. And why should it? It is always concerned with *anthropos teleios,* the *whole* man, even where, as in the Sermon on the Mount, the decalogue is pressed home to refer to inward disposition. It is quite unbiblical to suppose that a "good intention" is enough. What matters is the whole good. . . . The "heart" in the biblical sense is not the inward life, but the whole man in relation to God. . . . That is why I am so anxious that God should not be relegated to some last secret place but that we should frankly recognize that the world and men have come of age, that we should not speak ill of man in his worldliness, but confront him with God at his strongest point.[5]

"The *whole* man in relation to God." A tonic word and a welcome one for all who would have religion be a virile fact. Bonhoeffer saw—as every clear-eyed observer is bound to see—that nearly everybody in the actual world is involved in what the narrowly pious might look down upon as "worldliness": making a living, attending to the everyday job, doing what has to be done by those who are members of a community and citizens. It is in the choices they make *there*— there where their preponderant energies are—that men must supremely find God. Not "services" on Sunday, but service for the common life out in the secular city through the main stream of the week is what matters most.

Conventional religion may forget that, and get real values twisted even at the moment when it assumes it is being most religious. Many American churches print their announcements for the week on stockforms devised and sold by some central agency, often with a device or picture on the cover

[4] *Ibid.,* p. 140.
[5] *Ibid.,* p. 160.

page that is supposed to give some proper message to the congregation. On one such weekly bulletin not long ago there was a color print of the interior of a church, with stained-glass windows, the people in the pews, the priestly garbed clergyman and the acolyte with his folded hands. The money offering was being brought up the aisle to be presented; and underneath the picture were these words— *Reasonable, Holy Living.* Which is exactly what the picture did not show—not yet. What was going on inside the stained glass windows could be *preparation* for living, but whenever it is suggested that religious exercises in themselves are "reasonable, holy living," then religion lets itself be cut off from the great arena of actual life.

Sometimes the failure of supposedly religious people to realize what "reasonable, holy living" ought to be is brought into shocking vividness by some sudden event. In Grenada, Mississippi, in the summer of 1966, a mob of white men attacked and beat Negro children who were trying to enter what had been a segregated school. A minister in that town, who had been an army chaplain and who had a flaming courage which not every so-called "man of God" possesses, denounced that outrage and called upon his congregation to kneel in corporate penance for the community's barbarity. And this is what he said about it.

"I looked out of my church study window and I thought, 'My God, what has the church been doing that this could happen?'

"Where was the church when these seeds of prejudice were sown? Such acts are born of attitudes. How could prejudice and stubborn resistance to change have been allowed to grow until they could burst into violence? The condemnation of the church was not on that Monday morning, but on all the mornings of the years gone by. If the church has nothing to say under those circumstances, what does the church ever have to say? We have been so busy growing and

taking in members and submerging ourselves in activities
that we have lost sight of our individual responsibilities to
witness every day to the faith that is in us."[6]

Religion which shall be directly related to the crucial
facts of actual life—that is the necessity which all who are
both conscientious and clear-thinking must acknowledge.
When any section of the church withdraws into an unrelated pietism and makes men suppose that in such retreat
they save their souls, it loses what it thought it saved. Bonhoeffer recognized this with a growing acuteness. It seemed
to him that for many churches, and for innumerable people
in them, their so-called Christianity had become not much
more than an introverted concern for personal salvation, an
ecclesiastical greenhouse devoted to the growing of some sort
of exotic spirituality supposed to have to do with heaven.
But our business, wrote Bonhoeffer, is to live completely
now. This world must not be prematurely written off. "The
Christian . . . does not need a last refuge in the eternal from
earthly tasks and difficulties. Like Christ himself . . . he must
drink the earthly cup to the lees, and only in his doing that is
the crucified and risen Lord with him, and he crucified and
risen with Christ." And because it seemed to Bonhoeffer that
too many people who ought to know that Christianity means
self-forgetting service in the world were actually retreating
from earthly tasks and difficulties, and thinking instead that
religion properly has to do with "sacred" contemplations, he
began to say that what we need is "religionless Christianity."
It was a phrase which had for him, and might have for
everybody, a powerful astringent value: a call to stop being
tied up in continual questions as to how our souls are getting
on, and to go out to play our part in a world of men and to
find our soul in action. If this is a time when man has "come
of age," then in order to bring us to our fulfillment God may
be teaching us that sometimes "we must live as men who can

[6] C. B. Burt, in *Look*, December 27, 1966.

get along very well without him."[7]

That is the positive meaning intended to be expressed in "religionless Christianity." But it is a form of words open to misunderstanding and misuse. The recommendation of religionless Christianity for man who has "come of age" might seem to suggest—and by some has been taken to say—that most of the beliefs which men have held about God and his relation to our life have been childish; and, furthermore, that since in practical matters many people seem to think that "everything gets along without God," therefore to arrive at maturity we had better leave God out of our accounting altogether. That is exactly what some contemporary writers do approve and recommend; but if leaving God out of account should be held to mean that everything we ultimately need can be arrived at through our bland self-assurance, then we had better listen to the stabbing words of T. S. Eliot:

> Can you keep the City that the Lord keeps not with you?
> A thousand policemen directing the traffic
> Cannot tell you why you come or where you go. . . .
> Though you forget the way to the Temple,
> There is one who remembers the way to your door:
> Life you may evade, but Death you shall not.
> You shall not deny the Stranger.[8]

If God were only a refuge and recompense for passive souls, and if reliance upon him meant only dependence and flabby goodness, it might indeed be better to get along without him in order to be grown up. But the blind spot here would be in failure to see what the relationship of the living God to the soul of man really is. The nature of that relationship shines out from what seems at first the curious contra-

[7] *Prisoner for God,* pp. 154, 164.
[8] "The Rock," from *Collected Poems 1909-1962* (New York: Harcourt, Brace & World, Inc, 1963). Used by permission of Harcourt, Brace & World, Inc. and of Faber and Faber Ltd.

diction between two sentences in the last chapter of St. Paul's Letter to the Galatians: "Bear ye one another's burdens, and so fulfil the law of Christ"; and then, "For every man shall bear his own burden."

How can both of those be true? If someone else is bearing my burden, what except weakness can come to me if I have no responsibility to bear it myself? And if I do bear my own burden, how does someone else bear it?

The answer is that bearing burdens can be a creative thing when it is mutual, when the one who helps, bears the burden not *for* me but *with* me. A boy comes to his father with a problem; a question in his school lessons which he does not know how to answer, or a decision which he does not know how to make. Suppose the father takes the schoolbook, the sum in arithmetic or the outline in geometry or whatever, figures out the answer and handing it back impatiently, says, "Here now, I've done it for you, so that's that" —then for the long run the boy is more hurt than helped. But suppose the father says, "Let's think it out together," and then leads the boy along in a gradual understanding until the boy's eyes brighten and he knows that the next time he can work out his problem by himself, then the relationship is deepened, and with that and because of that the boy is made able to go forward on his own. That is the way it is in human contacts at their best; and that is the way it ought to be and can be between the human soul and God. The One who has made us for himself, and is the Life within our life, can be to us both illumination and encouragement, and at the same time make us more fit to carry our responsibilities as his adult sons.

Another danger also is lurking in the idea of a "religionless Christianity," an idea which Bonhoeffer's questing thought explored, but which some of the "radical theologians" have fastened upon as though it were an ultimate conclusion. The aversion to letting religion be only introspective and self-serving is sound and right, but that fear exaggerated could lead to a reaction which would cut the real human self in two. It is true that concern for one's own personal salvation can become so controlling that our conception of God and of his value for us is made narrow and self-absorbed and mean. But always it is a fact that if man is in any sense an eternal soul and not a mere knot of temporary energies he has an inner life which needs to be redeemed. Who is there that will not echo out of his confession these words which have been written in our immediate time?

Each one of us carries around inside himself, I believe, a certain emptiness—a sense that something is missing, a restlessness, a deep feeling that somehow all is not right inside his skin. Psychologists sometimes call it anxiety, theologians sometimes call it estrangement, but whatever you call it, I doubt that there are very many who do not recognize the experience itself, especially no one of our age, which has been variously termed the age of anxiety, the lost generation, the beat generation, the lonely crowd. Part of the inner world of everyone is this sense of emptiness, unease, incompleteness, and I believe that this in itself is a word from God, that this is the sound that God's voice makes in a world that has explained him away. In such a world, I suspect that maybe God speaks to us most clearly through his silence, his absence, so that we know him best through our missing him.[9]

Sooner or later and somehow human beings may begin to ask themselves: "What is the purpose of my life?" "What's wrong with me?" "What lies beyond death?"—though, as has been pointed out, it is a curious thing that none of these questions comes to the fore in such a book as *Honest to God*.[10] And some of the contemporary spokesmen of "radical theology" would dismiss these ultimate questions as of no important concern to this twentieth-century world. "Augus-

[9] Frederick Buechner, *The Magnificent Defeat* (New York: Seabury Press, 1966), p. 48.
[10] Fenton Morley, in *The Honest to God Debate* (London: SCM Press, 1963), p. 47.

tine has sung lyrically and soothingly to many, 'restless is
our heart until it comes to rest in Thee.' Our response today
is, maybe some hearts are, and maybe some are not."[11] And
if there are some hearts which hunger for an answer to those
questions, even so is there any need for God? Not according
to those who think they speak for the modern man. "There
are problems and needs, to be sure," writes William Hamilton, "but the world itself is the source of the solutions, not
God. God must not be asked to do what the world is fully
capable of doing: offer forgiveness, overcome loneliness,
provide a way out of despair, break pride, assuage the fear
of death. These are worldly problems for those who live
in this world, and the world itself can provide the structures to meet them."[12]

Ralph Waldo Emerson listened once on a winter's day to a
preacher discoursing on a theme that seemed to have no life-
blood in it. By contrast even the weather outside seemed
warmer than his words. "The snowstorm was real," wrote
Emerson, "the preacher merely spectral, and the eye felt the
sad contrast in looking at him and then out of the window
behind him into the beautiful meteor of the snow. He had no
word indicating that he had laughed or wept, was married
or in love, had been commended or cheated or chagrined. If
he had ever lived or acted, we were none the wiser for it. . . .
The capital secret of his profession, to convert *life* into truth,
he had not learned."

Who can say that truth has come out of life when it is said
that the *world* can "offer forgiveness, overcome loneliness,
provide a way out of despair, break pride, assuage the fear
of death"? Is that reality, or only spectral academic talk?
Tell the man who is agonizing in bitter remorse for some
great love which he has wounded and for which it is too late

---

[11] William Hamilton, in Altizer and Hamilton, *Radical Theology and the
Death of God* (Indianapolis: Bobbs-Merrill, 1966), p. 117.
[12] *Ibid.*, p. 116.

now for him to seek forgiveness; tell the man who faces the awful loneliness of having lost the one who was most precious to him; tell the man for whom some shattered hope has turned into near-despair; tell the man near to death who says "so much to do, so little done"—that *the world* can give him all he needs, and hear what he will say! He may or may not believe that there *is* an Everlasting Mercy to which he can turn, but he will know that nothing less than that is what his heart cries out for. He will not be gulled into thinking that flat words of the world can help him. He must have a Word from something great enough to call it God.

When God is lost, a brightness goes out of the sky. The brilliant young writer, Katherine Mansfield, said in a letter to her husband, "There's no God. That is queer. If only one could make some small grasshoppery sound of praise to *someone*—thanks to someone. But who?"

And in another letter she wrote: "It seems to me there is a great change come over the world since people like us believed in God. God is now gone for all of us. Yet we must believe; and not only that—we must carry our weakness and our sin and our devilishness to somebody. I don't mean in a bad abasing way. But we must feel that we are *known*, that our hearts are known, as God knew us."[13]

"I am thinking," wrote A. Leonard Griffith, minister of the City Temple, London, of those people who have believed in

a God who created us and cares for us, who sent his Son to redeem us, a God who answers prayer and to whom we go when we die. . . . I have been a garden-variety preacher and pastor counselling people in their troubles, comforting them in their sorrows and helping them to face death unafraid. What new language must I now employ? . . . . "The eternal God is thy refuge,

[13] From Katherine Mansfield's letters as published by Alfred A. Knopf, quoted in Henry Sloane Coffin's *Joy in Believing* (New York: Charles Scribner's Sons, 1956), p. 13.

and underneath are the everlasting arms"—symbolic language to be sure, but how else mediate the comfort and strength of God to a person about to undergo surgery? Many years ago, in a poor district of Aberdeen, a Unitarian minister preached to an open-air congregation a message that left out the saving Gospel of the Cross. A prostitute standing nearby said to him, "Your rope is not long enough for me." . . . The God "out there" has let down a very long rope . . . to the lowest depths of our misery and sin. So I cling to that rope with both hands, and God help me if I ever let go.[14]

If there is any substance in the idea that "the world" can satisfy the needs of the souls of men, the world must mean the human fellowship. Certainly no material things, no impersonal events, no changes of the weather, no blind forces in earth or sea or sky, can minister profoundly to the inner spirit. It is true that the comradeship of other men and women does help—helps against loneliness and despair. But it can help only in a partial way. For all other human beings are like ourselves: finite and limited, and moving on—as we are—to inevitable death. When the utmost that we can give to one another is completed, what *meaning* is there for us and for them if all alike go down to ultimate extinction, and there is nothing at the heart of the universe that cares for human souls?

"Religionless Christianity" was one of the paths—or by-paths—which the thought of Dietrich Bonhoeffer followed as he sought to chart his convictions—as an explorer draws parts of a map which may be tentative because there was not time enough in which it might have been made complete. But some of the radical contemporary thinkers, and also Bishop Robinson, have been so fascinated by the newness of this bypath that they have committed themselves to it as though it were the one sure way into Bonhoeffer's central thought and his witness to our world. What he has said

[14] *The Honest to God Debate,* p. 104.

about man "come of age," and called to adult responsibilities in which sometimes he must "get along without God," has been treated as though he meant that nothing besides our own self-sufficiency matters, and that if God should be dead there would be no special loss. But what Bonhoeffer did mean was different, and far deeper. He wanted men to find God by finding the heroic possibilities within themselves which it was God's supreme purpose to develop. He saw that it could be the love of God—and not any lack of God—that might seem to leave a man to face the tragic realities of life alone, so that out of the tragedy might come the spiritual triumph. That was the way it had been with Christ, who was willing to be deprived of all power on the cross—and find on the other side the Resurrection.

To say that this was and is the message of Bonhoeffer is certified by the one who knew him best. As these words are written, Eberhard Bethge, Bonhoeffer's beloved friend to whom many of the letters from prison were written and by whom the *Letters* were edited and made public, has been giving his emphatic testimony to what the real facts are. Brought to the United States by Union Theological Seminary in New York, he has spoken to many groups about the man he knew. Here is the opening paragraph of the report by a religious editor of what Dr. Bethge said on February 22, 1967.[15]

"The common notion that Dietrich Bonhoeffer taught or believed in the 'Death of God' is wrong, the German martyr's friend, biographer, editor, and best-known interpreter declared today at Western Maryland College."

And Eberhard Bethge went on to interpret what it was that Bonhoeffer wanted when he spoke of a "religionless Christianity." He was thinking—as we have already recognized—of deliverance from the withdrawn and feeble piousness which had come to mean religion for many in the offi-

[15] Weldon Wallace, in the Baltimore *Sun*, February 22, 1967.

cial German church, "an establishment which privileged people joined in order to maintain their bourgeois respectability," a selfish reaching out for a soft heaven—a Sunday religion, with no taut purpose to carry a spiritual commitment into the secular realities which men have to deal with every day. "God must be found at the *center* of life."

It is ironic that Bonhoeffer, who wanted God at the center of life, should have been interpreted—and misinterpreted— as skeptical of God's real presence anywhere. No one who reads the whole of *Prisoner for God*, and not merely some of the tentative questions which his ranging thought pursued, can fail to feel the positive power of his living faith.

"The responsible man seeks to make his whole life a response to the question and call of God," he wrote in "After Ten Years"; and again: "I believe that God both can and will bring good out of evil. For that purpose he needs men who make the best of everything. . . . I believe that even our errors and mistakes are turned to good account. . . . I believe God is not just timeless fate but that he waits upon and answers sincere prayer and responsible action."

In December, 1943, he wrote from his prison to his father and mother:

For a Christian there is nothing peculiarly difficult about Christmas in a prison cell. I daresay it will have more meaning and will be observed with greater sincerity here in this prison than in places where all that survives of the feast is its name. That misery, suffering, poverty, loneliness, helplessness and guilt look very different in the eyes of God from what they do to man, that God should come down to the very place which men usually abhor, that Christ was born in a stable because there was no room for him in the inn—these are things which a prisoner can understand better than anyone else. For him the Christmas story is glad tidings in a very real sense. And that faith gives him a part in the communion of saints, a fellowship transcending the bounds of time and space.

Again and again in his letters there is reflected the inspiration which Christian worship had had for him; and lovely memories of special days and seasons ring in his recollection like the sound of golden bells.

I can still hear the hymns we sang in the morning and evening, "Praise to the Lord, the Almighty, the King of Creation. . . . Shelters thee under his wings, yea, and greatly sustaineth." How true it is and may it ever remain so!

In times like these [at Christmas] we learn as never before what it means to possess a past and a spiritual heritage untrammelled by the changes and chances of the present. A spiritual heritage reaching back for centuries is a wonderful support and comfort in face of all temporary stresses and strains.

Today is Ascension Day, and a day of great joy for all who believe that Christ rules the world and our lives.

And writing to a little child in a family he loved, who was about to be baptized, he expressed his sense of the timeless value that may be in the familiar things, which only to the careless need become conventional:

There are certain fundamental truths about human life to which men will always return sooner or later. . . . The piety of your home will not be noisy or loquacious, but you will be brought up to say your prayers and to fear God above all things, to love him and to do the will of Jesus Christ.

In one of the last letters which came from him he wrote:

Please don't ever get anxious or worried about me, but don't forget to pray for me—I'm sure you don't! I am so sure of God's guiding hand, and I hope I shall never lose that certainty. You must never doubt that I am travelling my appointed road with gratitude and cheerfulness. My past life is replete with God's goodness, and my sins are covered by the forgiving love of Christ crucified. I am thankful for all those who have crossed my path, and all I wish is never to cause them sorrow, and that they like me will always be thankful for the forgiveness and mercy of God and sure of it.[16]

The British officer who was in the prison with Bonhoeffer when he was summoned to his execution has left this record:

Sunday 8th April, 1945, Pastor Bonhoeffer held a little service and spoke to us in a manner which reached the hearts of all, finding just the right words to express the spirit of our imprisonment and the thoughts and resolutions which it had brought. He had hardly finished his last prayer when the door opened and two evil-looking men in civilian clothes came in and said, "Prisoner Bonhoeffer, get ready to come with us." Those words "come with us"—for all prisoners they had come to mean one thing only—the scaffold.

We bade him good-bye—he drew me aside—"This is the end," he said. "For me the beginning of life."[17]

For such a life and such a consummation of it, could "religionless" ever seem to be the rightly expressive final word? No. Not from "the world" can come the quietness, strength and courage that fortify a man's soul, and make it true for him that at the crossing of the river "all the trumpets sounded for him on the other side." And it is not from any argument, but from the witness of such a spirit as that of Bonhoeffer, that there comes a flaming contradiction to the gray idea that "God is dead."

[16] *Prisoner for God,* pp. 21, 28, 58, 59, 135-136, 185.
[17] *Ibid.,* p. 11.

# V

## The Approach to God through Jesus

A GOD who is the Ground of Being, and is apprehended also as the Power that makes for Righteousness in and through the long drama of history, might conceivably seem to be the answer to men's search for the ultimate Reality. But as a matter of fact that is not true. Here we are, we human beings, created by something or Someone greater than ourselves: with minds that think long thoughts and hearts which are capable of loving. The highest instincts implanted in us reach out to find their larger likeness in that which made us what we are: not toward an impersonal process, but toward a spiritual Presence more wonderful and more warm.

In a church magazine in 1966 there was a brief account by a New York business man of something that happened to him one day in the concourse of the Pennsylvania Railroad Station as he was in a crowd just starting to go through the gates to a train. A man coming from another direction looked at him, stopped, and said to him:"You have the face of a man who might care about people. I am a convict just out of prison, who makes no difference much to anybody. But it would help me if I could think that you would remember me some time." And before the first man could stop him, he was gone.

Someone who cares, and who remembers. That is what every human being craves. Once there was an answer to that craving, an answer so vivid and so special that the whole world which experienced it seemed different. What we think of as the Christian faith reaches out to ranges of meaning beyond our utmost measurement. But it all began in something near and personal and intimate. It began because somebody cared, and made men wonder then why he cared, and what his caring came from.

One day a man stood on the strand of a lake where some fishing boats were coming in to shore. The lake was in the province of Galilee, in Palestine, which then the Romans ruled. By the reckoning of the calendar, it was a long time ago; but in the link between what happened then and what continues now it is as though there had been no time at all between. For the four men in the boats were Simon—afterward to be called Peter—and Andrew his brother, and James and his brother John; and the one on the shore was Jesus.

Doubtless he had been there before, for Nazareth where he lived was not far from the lake, and he was no stranger to the men who were coming in from fishing. As the carpenter of Nazareth, he had a natural entrance into relationship with them, because he knew, as they did, what it meant to have work to do and to do it with strength and skill. He was part of their world of men who carried everyday responsibilities and understood the meaning of them. In Nazareth, and perhaps also in Capernaum, he had cut the beams and shaped the doors of houses, turned the wood of yokes and smoothed them so that they might lie easy on the necks of oxen, mended the broken things that women brought him or the toy that a little child put trustfully into his hands. In the countryside his quick interest took in all the facts that might have seemed to be only the routine of dull existence, but through which also a larger life of mind and heart might find expression: a shepherd going after a lost sheep, a man plowing a field and sowing seed in steady trust that the grain would grow, a woman kneading leaven into flour or bringing water from the well. If he went out with the fishing fleet he would have the same quick imagination and the same relationship to life which he had everywhere, so that—as one of the Gospels would afterward describe—he could be more alert than others to see where the fish were running, and be the kind of companion who could make men like Simon and Andrew and James and John more confident about everything when he was in the boat.

Such was the man of Nazareth whom Simon and the others saw waiting for them on the shore of the lake that day. Such at least he was in those aspects which were already most familiar. But there were other facts about him which they did not yet know so well. His thoughts had ranged beyond the scenes of Nazareth and Capernaum. On the highroads of Galilee, the Way of the Sea that ran from Damascus to the port on the Mediterranean which the Romans had built at Ptolemais and down the coast to Egypt, and the great road to the East and Arabia, Jesus had watched the world's wide life go by: camel trains from Palmyra and Baghdad, herdsmen driving flocks of sheep, merchants convoying precious cargoes, Roman legions with the eagles of imperial dominion flashing in the sun. But through and beyond that pageant his thought had reached to that which could have a mightier meaning. In the quiet of the hills of Nazareth he had meditated on God and on what might be the will of God. In the crowding commotion of the roads were the mingled energies of life: its eagerness and vigor, its pursuit of those necessities which human beings are obliged to strive for, and at the same time its greed, its passions, its hard thrust for selfish power. No great purpose was binding it together, or shaping it to a creative end. But what if there should be a kingdom of the spirit in which men could find their larger selves, and because of which all that each man is in himself and all that men must do together can begin to have eternal worth? That was the mighty vision which Jesus saw, wide as the world and reaching to the end of time. But the reality of it could begin where any man responded. And that was what Jesus had come to the Lake of Galilee to make men he cared for understand.

"Come with me," he said to Simon and Andrew and James and John. Other than that, no lengthy explanation. "Come with me." What for? Where to? They did not know, and apparently they did not stop to ask. There was a fascination about him to which something in all of them responded. So they folded up their nets, beached their boats, and went with him. It was as simple and direct as that.

On the Sabbath day they were in the synagogue in Capernaum. Jesus was preaching to the people about the Kingdom of God, which he said was now at hand. They did not know altogether what he meant, but they saw what he did. In the synagogue there was a man who was demented. The congregation might have wanted nothing but to get rid of him, but Jesus went to him, held him with his eyes, and spoke to him; and the man's wildness vanished and he was himself again. The news of this spread fast. Here was someone who not only looked at human suffering, but also did something about it. It was no wonder then that before the sun went down that evening great numbers of sick folk were crowding outside the door of the house where Jesus was. "He healed many who were sick with various diseases, and cast out many demons," says the Gospel of Mark. "The force which Jesus had," writes the twentieth-century scholar, Joseph Klausner, no Christian but orthodox Jew, "comprises some secret, some mystical element, still not properly studied by the ordinary psychologists and physicians and scientists who are conversant with the laws of nature so far determined by science."[1] The pathetic people who flocked around Jesus in Capernaum did not know the "secret" in his healing either. All they knew was that they had come into touch with a great compassion which had power.

Persons "possessed by demons" or " with an unclean spirit" are phrases used to identify some of those whom Jesus healed. The words may be dated, but the facts are not. Human lives do get invaded by forces which can seem demonic: bewilderments, anxieties, fears which come—like the evil spirits described in one of Jesus' parables who crept into an empty house—to take possession of the mind and drive the real man out. In Palestine of that first century, impoverished and resentful, there were many so distraught that they were treated as insane. Such persons might be terrifying, like the mad man of Gadara described in the fifth chapter of Mark, "who lived among the tombs and no one could bind him any more, even with a chain." But even to this wild creature Jesus brought a saving power which the mad man recognized when he first saw him—the power of a pity that reached out to find a human soul and to set it free.

When the little group of men who had first begun to follow Jesus looked at him as he went out among all sorts of people, they could see with their own eyes what he gave to everybody and understand the fact he had expressed when he said one day that he had come that they might "have life and have it abundantly." Anyone who came in contact with him could recognize, all of a sudden, what it could mean really to be alive—alive to the wonder right there in the common things around them, and alive to the worthwhileness of ordinary human beings who might have seemed of no consequence whatever.

After the spring rains the Palestinian fields were ablaze

[1] *Jesus of Nazareth* (New York: The Macmillan Company, 1927), p. 270.

with flowers. But what of it? the disciples may have thought. Every year the whole lot of them springs up, and in a day or two they are all gone. What difference do they make? But Jesus looked at them with a great light in his eyes. Solomon in all his glory was not as magnificent as these, he said. Here is the lavishness of God, who pours out his gifts even on that which perishes. How much more will he give to his children, if they look to him in faith!

One day the disciples stopped by a village common. Was anything important there? Not according to their idea. Nothing and nobody except some noisy children playing. Brush them aside—and don't let them come bothering Jesus. Nothing there on the village common except some children playing? Look again! There in those children playing is the lift of the spirit, the bright imagination, the blessed youthfulness out of which alone can be built the Kingdom of God.

On another day Jesus came to a crossroads where a man named Matthew had his tax-collector's booth; and, being a tax-collector, had no faintest notion that anybody who was concerned about religion would have any special use for him. His business was collecting the tribute money on commission; and the more he could collect, even if it meant squeezing the poor, and grafting if he could on the well-to-do, the better off he would be. But when Jesus stopped and looked at Matthew, Jesus saw in him what Matthew did not know was there: a different sort of somebody altogether, a man who was meant for something better than his shady occupation. Jesus said to him exactly what he had said to Simon and Andrew and James and John, "Come with me." And Matthew tumbled out of his booth and followed. He said he wished Jesus might come to his house, but he supposed of course that Jesus wouldn't, because his—Matthew's —friends were not the most reputable people of the town. But Jesus said, Why not? "I have not come to call the righteous, but sinners." So he went and sat down with the crowd who had been sinners but were ready to try to be something else when they had seen Jesus; and as Dorothy Sayers in *The Man Born to Be King* has made Matthew say, "And nobody seemed surprised, only me."[2]

Another time, a Pharisee named Simon—the same name as the first of the disciples, but a very different person— invited Jesus to have dinner with him; and while he was there in Simon's house a woman who had been linked notoriously with many men came in without anyone in Simon's household seeing her in time to keep her out. She fell on her knees where Jesus was, broke into a flood of tears, and poured out upon his feet a vial of precious perfume. Simon was scandalized. Didn't Jesus know "what manner of woman" this woman was? But Jesus understood the passion of her repentance. Her sins, though they had been many, were forgiven. Mary Magdalene, whose presence in his house the Pharisee was ashamed of, had become for Jesus a life made white again, a soul redeemed into which as through a golden gateway the grace of God was coming in.

All these things the disciples saw, and one thing above all else they were certain of: Jesus cared. He cared for everybody who was in trouble—and for those also who ought to have been troubled but hadn't yet waked enough to their inner needs to know it. Once when he was journeying he stopped to rest by Jacob's well, and there came a woman of Samaria to get water. All she had in her mind was the daily drudgery of bringing her water jars, dragging up enough from the well to fill them, carrying the heavy weight of them home—and then the same thing tomorrow, and the day after that. If anyone could break that monotonous round for her, it would be all she asked. But Jesus made her aware of something else—aware of an inner thirst that could not be satis-

[2] London: Victor Gollancz, 1943, p. 122.

fied at Jacob's well, an inner need for purity and peace of
soul to which he said he would give living water so that she
would never thirst again.

In Jesus, as we read about him and think about him, there
is the sovereign quality of full life.

Most of us escape so much by being less than fully alive, but he
seems to escape nothing. . . . Always, with all of himself, he seems
to be vulnerable to all of it and especially to the pain that is
around him, not just the pain of the crippled and the bereaved,
but the slow, unspoken pain of being human. "Come unto me, all
ye that labor and are heavy-laden, and I will give you rest." And
he means everybody because everybody labors and is heavy-
laden—Pilate, Judas, Albert Schweitzer, Marilyn Monroe, Adolf
Eichmann.[3]

Meanwhile the disciples were beginning to be more and
more aware of what was happening in themselves. Jesus had
become the center of their whole existence. He was making
them into bigger men than they had ever been before. He
had said one day to the first of the four fishermen, "So you
are Simon the son of John? You shall be called Peter—which
means a Rock." "Me a rock?" the astonished Simon may have
echoed. He knew that at that moment he was a long way
from any such description: well-meaning, yes, and eager and
impulsive, but never sure that in any crisis he would have
the steady mind and the stout heart that could be depended
on. All the same, Jesus had said that he might amount to
something; not the old Simon merely, but the new Peter who
should be fit to be Jesus' friend. *That* he would try to be.
And that was what Matthew, who had been the tax collec-
tor, would also try to be. And so would Thomas and Philip
and Bartholomew and Simon the Zealot and the rest of the
twelve men whom Jesus chose to be closest to himself. They
loved him for what he was, and because he had first loved

[3] Frederick Buechner, *The Magnificent Defeat* (New York: Seabury Press,
1966), p. 93.

them: loved them notwithstanding their ordinariness, and notwithstanding that they would often disappoint him. But he, their Master, never disappointed them, nor ever fell short of a greatness that they would not have been able to believe in until they saw it in him. He could understand all sorts of people better than they understood themselves, and reach out to answer their unspoken needs. He had infinite compassion for all who were sad—and for all who had sinned and were sorry for it and ashamed; but also he could be terrible to the self-righteous and the hypocritical. There was a royalty in his bearing which made his disciples feel that nothing they could think about him could be greater than what would prove to be the fact. James and John came to him one day and showed what their imagination kindled to when they made their excited plea: "Grant us to sit, one at your right hand and one at your left, in your glory!" And Simon Peter already had voiced the tremendous expectation which Jesus had waked in him. At Caesarea Philippi Jesus had asked the disciples what the people were saying about him, and they had told him. Some said he was a prophet, some said he was Elijah come again, some said he was John the Baptist risen from the dead. "Who do you say that I am?" he asked them. Then it was that Peter cried, "You are the Christ!" That is to say, he was the ultimate One to whom the hope and faith of Israel through all the centuries had looked forward, the Messiah, the Deliverer, who would bring God's Kingdom to the earth.

They did not know yet what that Kingdom meant. Some thought of its coming in terms of the violence by which earthly kingdoms rise and fall; which for Israel of that first century would mean the letting loose of power from on high that would smash the rule of Rome and set the Chosen People free. And in every century men's instinctive desire may move in that same direction. It would be so convenient to have a miracle by which all that we resent in our conditions may be got rid of, and the world adjusted to our satisfaction —without too much personal cost and pain. But that was not what Jesus knew. The Kingdom of God, which is righteousness and peace, can come only to those who are ready to be made fit to welcome it—to men who want to be better in themselves and more responsible in service to one another. Often the world—or most of it—does not want that kind of Kingdom of the spirit, and will reject the one who could make it real. That is why, when Peter declared that Jesus was the Christ, Jesus answered—to Peter's shocked amazement—that "the Son of man must suffer many things, and be rejected by the elders and the chief priests and the scribes, and be killed, and after three days rise again" (Mark 8:11).

It is recorded in the Gospel of John (14:8) that the disciple Philip said to Jesus, "Lord, show us the Father, and we shall be satisfied." What was in Philip's mind was what has been in the mind of many another man before and since. "If we could just once see God himself in action, know of a certainty who he is and where his power is, then we could be confident. But where is anything big enough and miraculous enough to be such a sure sign of God that we cannot have a question any more?" So speaks the voice of our dull perception. And what did Jesus answer? "Have I been with you so long and yet you do not know me, Philip? He who has seen me has seen the Father." Which is to say that the world does not have to wait for some portent in order to recognize the presence of God. The presence of God and the power of God, the only sort of power which can actually enter into and redeem the minds and souls of men, is the spirit that was in Jesus.

The disciples, like the rest of us, were often slow to understand. But they began to *feel* the truth, no matter if they could not always express it fully. When the love of Jesus laid hold on them and began to make them over into better men, they knew that this was what the whole world needed in order to be made better too. He was for them the revelation of life as it was divinely meant to be. So they followed him in spite of the plain fact that often they were afraid. They went up to Jerusalem with him, thinking at first that he was going to a triumph, but *wanting* to be faithful even if and when there might be no triumph, but only defeat and death.

Thus the love of Jesus for the men who were his disciples, and their answering love for him, could lead them a long way. Other emotions could also lead men a long way, and in an opposite direction. If to the disciples and to many of the common people Jesus' message of the Kingdom of God brought enlargement of life, there were those on the other hand, scribes and Pharisees, who were instantly hostile to what he had to say. The kind of righteousness to which he summoned men cut across their interest and advantage. The Kingdom of God was all very well as long as it had to do with established religion—and the rewards of religion. Who had any right to question their religious eminence, when they were ushered to the chief seats in the synagogue and when even in the market place the people made way for them because of their ecclesiastical rank? Who was this Jesus out of Nazareth who dared to say that some of their seeming holiness was only a cloak for greed and cruelty; that they "devoured widows' houses and for a pretence made long prayers" (Matthew 23:13, note); and that common sinners might come from the east and west and north and south to find their way into the Kingdom of God while they—or some of them anyhow—would be cast out? And what would become of the prerogatives of Israel and the superiority of the Chosen People if the common crowd which this Jesus associated with, the "publicans and sinners," and even despised Samaritans, had to be treated as though they mattered as much to God as those like themselves who kept every jot and tittle of the law?

So it was no wonder that Pharisees and scribes in their

jealous churchmanship watched Jesus angrily, and were ready to join forces with any who would bring him to account. Nor were they lacking for allies. Herod, tetrarch of Galilee, would be as glad to get rid of Jesus' moral challenge as his wife had been glad to get rid of John the Baptist. The High Priests in Jerusalem, who had made terms with the Roman overlords, were afraid of him because they said he "stirred up the people"; and they, as guardians of the public order, were responsible to see that nothing inconvenient should be stirred up.

When in the week of the Passover Jesus came from Galilee to Jerusalem, a great crowd of those who had come from everywhere as pilgrims to the Feast met him on the Mount of Olives just outside the city walls. They had heard of him as the prophet from Nazareth concerning whom many wonders were reported. Now the word spread that this might be the Messiah! Therefore the multitude thronged about him, tore down palm branches and spread them on his road, and shouted their passionate acclaim: "Hosanna to the son of David! Blessed be he who comes in the name of the Lord." And the sound of their welcome, and the threat of it, came to the ears of the priests and the other authorities in Jerusalem who had counted him dangerous already.

From that day, events moved swiftly toward their fateful climax. On the day following, Jesus went to the Temple. There he was outraged to see its courts filled with noisy huckstering: traders with their penned-up animals and their pigeons on sale for the Temple sacrifices, money-dealers getting their fat commissions for changing ordinary money into the privileged currency which alone was permitted for "sacred" use. What was supposed to be a house of prayer looked more like a market place; and the worst of it was that the traders established there had bought their franchises by payments to the ruling priests. The wrath of Jesus flamed. He upset the tables of the money-changers, and drove out the rest of the hucksters and what they had to sell. He who could be so gentle that mothers brought their little children to his arms was terrible now as he confronted the protected greed which he said had made the house of God into "a den of thieves."

In the Passion Play at Oberammergau there is a dramatic scene which portrays what may actually have happened next. Caiaphas, the High Priest, goes to the Roman procurator, Pontius Pilate, to tell him that he may bring before the procurator a disturber of the peace, and that he hopes that Pilate will dispose of him without delay. When the Roman coldly refuses to commit himself, Caiaphas tells him that he will find out soon enough the forces he must confront if he refuses. And then the High Priest goes out to rouse and rally not only those who had been driven out of the Temple but all the other business interests—the Chamber of Commerce of Jerusalem, so to speak—who wanted no disturbance, and in whose eyes Jesus could seem a mortal enemy to their entrenched advantage.

Meanwhile, within Jesus' own inner company, there was defection. Judas Iscariot, one of the Twelve, had become embittered. Apparently he had thought, as Peter and the others may also have thought at first, that if Jesus were the Messiah he would come as a conqueror, to rouse Israel, to lead a Holy War of liberation and to break the power of Rome. Now that there was no sign of this, Judas, in his disillusionment, would avenge himself upon the Master by whom he began to think he had been deceived. So he went to Caiaphas, and to Annas who had also been High Priest, and offered to sell them information as to how and where Jesus could most quietly be seized.

Three days went by after the cleansing of the Temple. Then came the Passover, and Jesus' Last Supper with his disciples, including Judas. "One of you will betray me," Jesus said; and as the horrified disciples began one by one to ask, "Lord, is it I?" Judas rose, and as the Gospel of John describes that moment in one tragic sentence, "he went immediately out, and it was night."

From the supper Jesus led the disciples with him to the Garden of Gethsemane. There the Temple guard, sent by Caiaphas and guided by Judas, seized him; and led him to Caiaphas' house for trial and for condemnation on the charge of blasphemy. However, it was not on that charge, but on a more adroitly chosen one, that Caiaphas and all the forces he had rallied presented Jesus to Pilate in his praetorium the next day. They said he was a threat to peace and order, that he claimed to be a king, and that "everyone who makes himself a king sets himself against Caesar." Thus Pilate was intimidated, for he knew that the deadliest accusation that could be brought to the emperor in Rome against one of his officials was that such an official had been tolerant of sedition. So, lest he himself be compromised, he handed Jesus over to be crucified.

That seemed to be the end. With a crown of thorns which mocking Roman soldiers had pressed down upon his head, Jesus was nailed to the central cross between two convicted robbers on the hill outside Jerusalem. "We had hoped that he was the one to redeem Israel," one of his obscure disciples was to say. But it did not appear then that there had been much redemption, or much evidence that any power of God had come significantly into the world.

Yet two things had happened. Notwithstanding the crucifixion, the world had not got rid of Jesus; and through him there had come a revelation of the reality of God and of the nature of God which would outlast death and time.

# VI

## Changing Thought and
## Unchanging Reality

THE preceding chapter began with the recognition that there is a longing in every human heart to know that there is someone who cares and will remember. Then thought turned to the fact that there was one who did care supremely: care for people, and care for the goodness that could make them into the kind of people they were meant to be. That one was Jesus; and the thought of Jesus still stirs the minds and warms the hearts of men. The Gospel story of his human life gets hold of the imagination—his passion for righteousness, his concern for people, his self-transcending devotion to the redeeming will of God, his steady commitment that would carry him all the way to his inevitable cross. Nearly every person, Christian believer or not, can feel the immense magnetism of Jesus.

"Jesus, yes—and that is just where the trouble begins," many might be inclined to say. "Jesus as a human figure, Jesus as a man among men, understanding us and understandable, we could be drawn to. But look what the fact is. He has been wrapped up in so many theological abstractions that the reality gets lost. If we go to church some time we may hear a creed recited which says that he was 'the only-begotten Son of God; Begotten of his Father before all worlds, God of God, Light of Light, Very God of very God; Begotten, not made; Being of one substance with the Father.' Preachers and Sunday school teachers speak about him as God come down to earth. If we have to say and think all that, what relationship can Jesus actually have to us?"

The impact of the question has been made the heavier by the blunt statements of two contemporary writers.

Certainly up to the Second World War, the commonest vision of Jesus was not as a human being *at all*. He was a God in human form, full of supernatural knowledge and miraculous power, very much like the Olympian gods were supposed to be when they visited the earth in disguise.[1]

. . . the traditional supranaturalistic way of describing the Incarnation almost inevitably suggests that Jesus was really God almighty walking about on earth, dressed up as a man, Jesus was not a man born and bred—he was God for a limited period taking part in a charade. He looked like a man, he talked like a man, he felt like a man, but underneath he was God dressed up. . . . However guardedly it may be stated, the traditional view leaves the impression that God took a space-trip and arrived on this planet in the form of a man. Jesus was not really one of us; but through the miracle of the Virgin Birth he contrived to be born so as to appear one of us. Really he came from outside.[2]

That is what many persons have supposed that they had to believe if they were to have any correct Christian belief at all, and as a result some who try to be honest with themselves may conclude that the whole thing is caught up in confusion, and that nothing intelligible can be arrived at,

---

[1] John Wren-Lewis, quoted in Robinson, *Honest to God* (Philadelphia: Westminster Press, 1963), p. 66.
[2] Robinson *op. cit.,* p. 66.

unless and until most of the old creeds and theological formulations have been scrapped and forgotten. "Let's get back to simplicity," the impatient may be tempted to exclaim. "We see the kind of goodness that was in Jesus. Try to follow that, and let the elaborate definitions about him go. That will be enough for modern man."

But as a matter of fact it will not be enough for "modern man," as it never has been enough for the profound needs of men in any time. And the reason is that it leaves unanswered the ultimate question which human souls are bound to ask. Where does the power of goodness come from, and what undergirds it at last? Paul the apostle wrote of Jesus that "God was in Christ reconciling the world to himself." Is that true? Or is it true, rather, that "God is dead," and always has been dead in the sense that there is not and never has been any transcendent reality such as Jesus believed overshadowed him? If that is so, then the spirit of Jesus was merely a forlorn and temporary flicker which the evolutionary process somehow managed to create, with nothing in the infinite to have kindled it, and therefore nothing to make it alive again for us.

Certainly it makes a difference to know which of those two possibilities was the fact. Therefore it is important to consider with thoughtfulness and imagination what the Christian creeds and confessions—even in those phrases which at first seem abstract—have been trying to express. All language, past or present, is imperfect. It has to use symbols and suggestions, which at best can only point to the experienced fact; and the experienced fact which lies back of everything that was said of Jesus was the tremendous feeling that in him men encountered the Spirit of God who was and is alive.

Think, then, in this perspective of what the New Testament records and the faith that grew out of them had to say.

What the first disciples felt and were sure of was that something great and new had come into their lives through Jesus. Being Jews, they expressed it in terms that were shaped by their whole heritage of thought. Since the days of the prophets there had been the mighty hope that some day there would appear the Messiah, a Savior and Deliverer who would establish a new Kingdom of the spirit in the world of men. It was this that Jesus seemed to them already to be bringing and it was this conviction that burst into flame in the heart and mind of Simon Peter on that day which we have remembered when Jesus asked the disciples what the people were saying about him, and then asked them, "Who do you say that I am?" "You are the Christ!" came Peter's awed reply. He had no clear idea of just how the Christ would be a Savior, but a sudden deep awareness told him that every hope and faith had a new dimension now because of all that he had seen in Jesus. Nothing seemed too great to believe about God and what might come from God.

The writer of the Fourth Gospel put the same sort of witness into another form of words. It seemed to him that always there had been coming to the souls of men the message of a higher world, out of infinity a Word concerning the meaning of life which often our poor selves would only dimly understand. In order really to understand it, we had to see it, and in Jesus men could see it. The heavenly purpose for what men redeemed might be was shown in what he was. "The Word was made flesh and dwelt among us, and we beheld his glory."

Then later in the development of Christian thinking there came other efforts to find the language that would convey what people had felt about Jesus and because of him had dared to believe about God. In the fourth and fifth centuries the church tried to put all this into the so-called Nicene and Chalcedonian creeds. Once again it had to use the patterns of thought and the phraseology which belonged to that particular time. Greek philosophy spoke of "substance," as meaning that which is essential and distinctive in any living being—and in the divine Being also. How should the church therefore express its faith that through Jesus men could become aware of, and in touch with, what God really is? They did it by saying that he was "of one substance with the Father"—not of *like* substance only, but of one and the same substance. To us those words sound abstract and remote, but what they meant to the men who used them was definite and vital. They felt and they wanted to proclaim this tremendous conviction: that in Jesus there was expressed what the heart of God actually is. We finite beings stand within a universe which has depths of mystery. We know that back of creation and back of all life there is a Reality greater than we are. What *is* it in its ultimate nature? Is it blind force, or is it a living Spirit? If it is not an indifferent process, but a purpose and a will, is that purpose merciful and compassionate? Men had seen in Jesus the power of love to take hold of men and to make them over. Can we dare to trust that he whom "we have seen with our eyes, have looked upon, and our hands have handled, of the Word of life" is an authentic clue to the nature of the Unseen? Projecting into the infinite what we have known in Jesus, can we believe that everything *there* will ultimately be revealed to be like what men knew in him? *That* is what the thinkers of the church said Yes to when they said that he was "of one substance with the Father."

Now the trouble is that "substance" is a category of thought which is no longer native to us as expressing essential reality. We think in more dynamic and less static terms. God is known as and where we trace the moving of his Spirit; and because of the Spirit which men saw in Jesus, they could say that "God was in Christ, reconciling the world to himself."

But it is not only a single word in the creed that brings us to a halt. The whole range of conceptions which used to be taken for granted has become for us a closed road. The men of the early Christian centuries thought instinctively of God as up somewhere above the sky. He was there, and we are here. Therefore if God was to come down into the life of men it had to be almost literally by what Bishop Robinson has called a "space-trip." That conception appears with classic vividness in John Milton's *Paradise Lost*. God the Father and God the Son confer in heaven. Adam and Eve have sinned, and therefore God declares concerning Adam:

> He with his whole posterity must die.
> Die he or justice must; unless for him
> Some other able, and as willing, pay
> The rigid satisfaction, death for death.

Then "all the heavenly choir stood mute, and silence was in Heaven"—until God the Son offered himself for man's redemption.

> Behold me then; me for him, life for life
> I offer; on me let thine anger fall;
> Account me man; I for his sake will leave
> Thy bosom, and this glory next to thee
> Freely put off, and for him lastly die.

God the Father accepts the offer of the Son, and sends him down to earth.

> I spare
> Thee from my bosom and right hand, to save,
> By losing thee awhile, the whole race lost.
> Thou, therefore, thou who only canst redeem,
> Their nature also to thy nature join;
> And be thyself man among men on earth,
> Made flesh, when time shall be, of virgin seed.
> By wondrous birth, be thou, in Adam's room,
> The head of all mankind, though Adam's son.

As in him perish all men, so in thee,
As from a second root, shall be restored
As many as are restored, without thee none.

Here is reflected the whole great theme of traditional theology: the sin of Adam and the fall of man, the wrath of God, the demand of heavenly justice that there must be an atonement for sin which humanity in its sinfulness could never make, and therefore the offer of God the Son to take humanity upon himself and offer an infinite sacrifice on its behalf. Here is "the plan of salvation," conceived as a mighty drama linking heaven and earth.

Profound values were in it—first of all the dignity which it gave to human souls. It looked upon life and destiny as no cheap and common thing, but as involved in eternal issues. And it believed in a God who cares.

Those values are part of an imperishable heritage. But the living truth simply will not come home to us now from within the ancient framework. We do not live in the conceptual world which John Milton pictured, and which was shaped by the instinctive ideas men had in the ages when they thought the earth was flat and heaven not far beyond the blue sky which arched above it.

What then *does* it mean to say that Jesus came from God, and that in his life the reality of God is manifest?

It means a recognition of God which *begins* with what we know and not in a supernatural realm we do not know. Some influences in life move on a level above a stodgy fleshliness, and when we are touched by them we are lifted up to where we breathe a wider and more quickening air. Or, to change the metaphor, we are conscious sometimes of depths within ourselves, which are like springs that can break through the arid ground—springs of thoughts and desires which in the moments of flat and dry existence we had not known were there. In that upper air, in those deep springs—use what simile you will—is God: God who is not off at a distance so that he has to be miraculously projected into our world, but God who from the beginning has been and is the creative Spirit. He is what Dietrich Bonhoeffer has expressed in one memorable phrase, "the beyond in the midst." Thus for every one of us it can essentially be true that in God "we live and move and have our being." The fact of what we experience is the cardinal matter. When we seek for language in which to express it, all terms will be symbolic and only approximate. Thinking of it in relation to our sense of the highest which we reach up to, it is as though we listened to One who says to us: "Thus saith the high and lofty One that inhabiteth eternity, whose name is Holy; I dwell in the high and lofty place, with him also that is of a contrite and humble spirit, to revive the spirit of the humble, and to revive the heart of the contrite ones." Or thinking in relation to our sense of the depths within ourselves which lie beneath our shallow consciousness, the same truth of an infinite Presence echoes in the words: "The eternal God is thy refuge, and underneath are the everlasting arms."

Consider now what this means for our conception of Jesus as the revelation of God and as God's "only Son." If we ourselves have been brought into existence not by the accidents of some blind physical force but by the creative consciousness of One who made us in his own image, then every human person is in some sense a child of God. Then also if one Person born into this our world of men were supremely attuned to the highest, completely open to and controlled by the Spirit of God, filled with the flame of a redemptive goodness of which other souls have only lesser sparks, he would be—in the living meaning of those words for us— God's only Son. *How* he became so might be expressed, and has been expressed, in forms of thought which embodied a wonder that could not be contained in common prose. So we have the lovely poetry of the first chapters of the Gospel of Luke, with their pictures of the annunciation angel appearing to the Virgin Mother, of the heavens filled with chanting angels above the plains of Bethlehem, of shepherds adoring at the manger, of majestic kings from the East bringing their gifts of gold and frankincense and myrrh. Later we have the imagery which Paul the apostle used, of "Christ Jesus, who, though he was in the form of God, did not count equality with God a thing to be grasped, but emptied himself, taking the form of a servant, being born in the likeness of men. And being found in human form he humbled himself and became obedient unto death, even death on a cross" (Philippians 2:8). (The same dramatic imagery of the Son coming down from heaven which John Milton put into the magnificence of *Paradise Lost.*) Later still the thinkers of the fourth and fifth centuries tried to find room for the experienced fact in great ranges of metaphysical interpretation, and so built the vast structures of the Nicene and Chalcedonian creeds. But all the while, and through all changing efforts to find explanatory words that would be adequate, the one living purpose was to help men look at Jesus of Nazareth and to know that "he that hath seen me hath seen the Father."

When Jesus and all that he meant and means is thought of thus in the way in which he actually comes home to the hearts and souls of men, it grows clear that Virgin Birth as a biological miracle has nothing to do with the experienced fact that in him God has been supremely apprehended. The faith and devotion of the apostle Paul was built on other foundations, and in nothing that he wrote is Virgin Birth so much as mentioned. The same is true of the Fourth Gospel. One who was at the time a troubled student has told of talking once with the wise and gentle William Newton Clarke of Colgate University, and of saying to him that he "could believe that Jesus was spiritually but not that he was physically divine. 'Physically divine?' said Dr. Clarke with a quizzical inflection. There was dead silence for a moment, and then I said: 'That is nonsense, isn't it?' 'Of course it is nonsense,' he answered; and then added in effect that if I would start by seeing that any divinity in Jesus must consist in his spiritual quality, I might get somewhere."[3] It was this "spiritual quality" that the first disciples knew; and the tradition of the Virgin Birth which grew up in the early church, and the beautiful story of Bethlehem in the Gospel of Luke, were the instinctive colors in which men pictured the infinite significance which Jesus had come to hold for them.

When put into such colors truth, and the living power of it, can be not less but more the truth. One remembers the illustration which Burnett H. Streeter used in one of his books. Writing of Venice, one of the most romantic cities of the earth, he asks how shall we best know its beauty and its wonder. One way would be to read a *Baedeker's Guide Book*, which lists the facts about Venice and its particular scenes with meticulous objectivity. Another way would be to look at one of the paintings in which J. M. W. Turner conveyed the over-all impression of that incomparable place. We might not be able to identify in his canvas any exact spot in Venice portrayed with photographic accuracy. But there in the glory of his coloring is the true Venice—its mood, its mystery, its timeless inspiration for those who come within its atmosphere. Similarly, the Gospel story of the birth in Bethlehem is written not with literalism, not in flat prose, but with a lift of the spirit that is like the lift of poetry; and its essential meaning has to do not with exactly how Jesus was conceived and born, but with the dimensions of significance which he had for the world into which he was born— and has for the world of today.

Therefore literal acceptance or nonacceptance of the traditional doctrine of the Virgin Birth is no criterion of Christian discipleship; and the same is true concerning some other forms of thought which have had immense value, but which

[3] Harry Emerson Fosdick, *The Living of These Days* (New York: Harper & Row, 1956), p. 56.

are not thereby made sacrosanct. Every thinker reflects the age in which he lives, and almost inevitably his interpretation of truth will be shaped by those human facts and the assumptions rising from them which men of his time take for granted.

In the early Christian centuries there was a vivid conception of the devil as "the prince of this world," within whose power mankind justly belonged because of human sin, to whom a ranson had to be paid, and that ransom was the death of Jesus. In a later period most of Europe was a feudal society; and in feudalism an offense against the feudal overlord could be wiped out only by satisfaction rendered by one of equal rank. Therefore the affront of man's sin to the holiness of God could be canceled, and the wrath of God turned aside, only if One who was himself God became man and by his sacrifice allowed what must otherwise have been God's implacable justice to be satisfied. That conception of the divine reality undoubtedly shaped the thought of Anselm when he wrote *Cur Deus Homo,* and established the particular doctrine of the atonement which has dominated the thinking of the Christian church from Anselm's time to this. For many centuries the Bible, including the story of Adam, was read as an infallible record, and all mankind regarded as condemned for Adam's sin and totally depraved. God meanwhile must be "the wholly Other," whose grace could come back into the world to save it only by some vertical projection, the Christ coming down as in *Paradise Lost* to redeem a human race which except for that exclusive incarnation could have had no link with God.

Conceptions such as those have lost their convincing power. Once they were the fabric of thought by which men's faith was warmed and protected as naturally as their bodies were warmed and protected by the clothing cut to the pattern of their time; but now those doctrines as they have been handed down have become strait-jackets in which the

present-day mentality cannot live. When preachers, or anybody else, interpret the nature of God and the needs of our
real world in the old dogmatic language, what they say
simply does not come alive; and that is why some, in their
impatience, have gone to the shrill extreme of declaring that
God himself is dead.

At the same time there is an opposite danger. The search
for more relevant religious language may lead to a shallow—
and even flippant—disparagement not only of old forms of
thought but also of the truth embodied in them.

The doctrine of original sin—whatever may have been the
outmoded methods of biblical interpretation which developed it—can help us look with a saving realism at the dark
areas of our human nature from which the instincts of the
jungle may so suddenly emerge.

The theologians of the Atonement and of the sacrifice of
Christ can bring home the realization that every wrong that
we commit may carry its vicarious involvement, that no sin
of ours is solitary, and that the most dire penalty for guilt
may be not the punishment we accept but the awful realization of the suffering we have laid upon the innocent.

To think upon the Otherness of God may humble our self-
complacency, and make us stand in awe before the ultimate
mysteries which confront our souls.

And to contemplate the doctrine of the Trinity, even
though our first impatience might want to dismiss it as a
riddle, can lead us along great avenues of spiritual understanding.

Granted that what we sometimes seem to see is not avenues, but a verbal thicket. The collect for Trinity Sunday in
the Book of Common Prayer confronts the would-be wor-
shiper with this:

Almighty and everlasting God, who hast given unto Thy servants grace, by the confession of a true faith, to acknowledge the
glory of the eternal Trinity, and in the power of the Divine Maj-

esty to worship the Unity; we beseech thee that thou wouldest keep us stedfast in this faith. . . .

"To acknowledge the glory of the eternal Trinity, and in the power of the Divine Majesty to worship the Unity"—for the average person those words, capital letters and all, may honestly seem not much more than sound. The impulse of worship which is seeking expression through them might find its way in simpler words, such perhaps as these:

O eternal God, Father, Son, and Holy Spirit, grant that in the majesty of all creation we may behold thy power that upholds us, in the face of Jesus Christ thy love that seeks and saves us, and in new life within our souls thy Spirit kindling in us; so that even in our littleness thine infinite wonder may be revealed, O blessed triune God.

But in any case, it would be a foolish loss to fail to recognize the agelong truth, and even superciliously to discard it, because we might not like the verbal wrapping. The Unity of God: that means the faith that the Reality our lives must deal with is not some inconsistent and capricious thing, but a saving will and purpose which we can depend upon and trust. And "the glory of the eternal Trinity" in its threefold living significance for us is this: that in the holy love of Jesus we have seen what the human heart longs for the nature of God to be; that through Jesus we have dared to believe that this is what God in his everlastingness *is*; and that all little glimmerings of goodness within ourselves come from the same Holy Spirit of God that was in Jesus.

Jesus. We keep coming back to that name. According to the Book of Acts, the apostle Peter declared in Jerusalem that "there is no other name under heaven given among men by which we must be saved." Is that true? And what does it mean?

It does *not* mean what is sometimes crudely thought. It does not mean that if a man responds to the invitation to "come forward" at a revivalist's meeting in the name of Jesus and "confess Christ," he is thereby "saved." Jesus is more than a name. He is reality, challenging and decisive.

Nor does the name of Jesus, and commitment to him as the Incarnation, mean something narrow, jealous and exclusive. Jesus of Nazareth was born at a particular time in human history. There had been a long span of life before him, as there has been after him. If the source of all existence is a living God, and if God is concerned for what he has created, then forever he must have been reaching out to all human souls. "In the beginning was the Word." Wherever there have been men sensitive to the Spirit, seers and prophets in any race and any time possessed by the intuition that life has meaning and that the meaning is redemptive, then gleams of the everlasting reality have come through. What the Christian faith holds concerning Jesus is that in him this meaning was supremely embodied and expressed. "The Word became flesh and dwelt among us." Not by his difference from the goodness which had been revealed before, but by his fulfillment of it, he is the Christ. To say that is to speak no theological abstraction. Neither is it to say something smooth and unrelated. It is to be confronted by a decision which is inescapable. Either the Christian faith is foolishness, or it is the truth upon which all life and destiny depend.

There are aspects in which its looks like foolishness. There is no use blinking that. Jesus died on a cross. Hard-boiled men who hated him and were contemptuous of the idea that "he saved others" pointed to the stark fact that "he cannot save himself." And that was true. The life which dared to summon the best that might be in men got instead the malignity of what was worst, because it is so hard for many men to face up to the challenge of being better than they already want to be. And it looked as though malignity had the final word. If there was any power in the kind of Kingdom Jesus had preached, then let him show it, "Let him come down from the cross."

He did not come down from the cross. In one sense love never can. It has to go on suffering as long as ignorance and evil last. But it takes the cross with it into a greater victory. Jesus crucified came back from death in living power to lay hold upon the hearts of men. It is not only those who call themselves Christians that feel his continual influence upon what they think, and upon what in conscience they have to try to do.

Here, and not in any lesser matters, is the recognition that is crucial. Many questions about Jesus have had their different answers, and always will. But one question is decisive. Is it, or is it not, when we look through his eyes that we know most surely what God is, and see the direction in which human life is meant to go?

"It is your Father's good pleasure to give you the kingdom." That is the promise which has come in the name of Jesus; and for those who make bold to trust it and live by it, his name may be indeed the only name by which we can be saved. For consider the profundity of meaning that lies in those words, like the depth of clear still water that reflects the stars. "Your Father." The Reality that undergirds the universe, then, is not blind process, but a beneficent Spirit who can be called by that personal name. There is something waiting to be given, which cannot be created by our own devices but which can begin to appear when men are responsive to the life that enfolds them and can flood into them as the tidal deeps of the ocean flood into the shallow bay. That gift is what Jesus called the Kingdom of God: a fellowship in which all men are of eternal worth because they are God's children, in which love is the way of life, and in which greatness is measured—as with Christ—not by what one gets but by what he gives.

Such a Kingdom of God may seem to be only an empty

notion to those who are ready to pour ashes, as at a funeral,
upon the agelong faith that the Infinite can be called "Our
Father." If so, the death-of-God movement might represent
instead the death of man—the death of those divinely given
intuitions which can reach up to great imagination and devotion, but which are smothered when life is content to be
nothing but flat and uninspired existence. "We must have . . .
faith in this world's final meaning and purpose, or we shall
become 'fed up' with life." But when a man takes seriously
the possibility of a Kingdom of God such as Jesus lived and
died for, then "he is on his way to find the great Reality to
which he can dedicate every power he possesses, and in
which he can find satisfaction for every fine desire of his
soul.[4]

This Kingdom to which the Christian tries to be committed has its foregleams now. Wherever there is sympathy
and gentleness and self-forgetting love, it is beginning to be
revealed. It does not have to wait for great occasions or for
some dramatic place. A young wife and mother whose days
were largely spent in the little things of home had seen its
meaning when she wrote: "Life in the kitchen and with the
children has been greatly enriched for me this winter because of the interpretation of the COMMONPLACES in life for a
Christian—and great joy has been added."

Out in the wider areas of the world also it will be by a
more commanding vision of God's Kingdom, and by that
only, that we may be saved. Colonel E. M. House, returning
from Paris after the tragic blunders of the Versailles Treaty
at the end of the First World War, said to Henry Sloane
Coffin: "In the midst of our discussions, the thought oc-
curred several times, 'If only we could stop and reflect what
would Christ think of this or that proposal, our discussion
would have been raised to a higher level, where solutions

[4] G. A. Studdert-Kennedy, *I Believe* (New York: George H. Doran Co.,
1921), p. 24.

might have been easier to reach and far wiser."[5] And in Maurice Hewlett's *The Life and Death of Richard Yea-and-Nay*,[6] one of the servants of Richard Coeur de Lion says to him:

"There was a Father, my lord King Richard, who slew His own Son, that the world might be the better."

"And was the world much better?" asked the monarch.

"Beau sire," came the reply, "not very much. But that was not God's fault, for it had, and still has, the chance of being the better for it."

[5] Henry Sloane Coffin, *Joy in Believing* (New York: Charles Scribner's Sons, 1956), p. 115.

[6] Toronto: Clapp, Clark & Co., 1900.

# VII

## The Human and the Divine

The world "had, and still has, the chance of being the better" because of Jesus. It "*still* has," in spite of the crucifixion. Men whose stubborn interests could not stand the presence of Jesus in their world had taken him to his cross, and thought—as we have remembered—that they had got rid of him forever. But they were wrong. On the third day after the crucifixion something happened which for his diciples was transfiguring. They said that Jesus had come back to them risen from the dead, invincibly alive.

It is impossible to draw from the stories in the Gospels any certain picture of the Resurrection, as it would be impossible to put on any canvas the unearthly colors of the aurora. In that mysterious borderland between life and death and that which lies beyond, who can say what may or may not be? The central fact, as summed up by one thoughtful New Testament scholar, was this at least: that the desolation which had followed the crucifixion was

overcome by spiritual dynamic of a more potent order. . . . The spiritual potency of Jesus, when death released him from earthly limitations, was able to present Him in His glorified state to

disciples whom He Himself had creatively prepared to receive
the revelation of His triumph over death. This religious experience and discovery, on which was based the primitive Church,
stands out clearly in its solidity, as a permanent datum of the
Gospel concerning Jesus Christ, by the side of which the more
doubtful elements such as the empty tomb and the inconsistent
evidence of the Gospels appear of a secondary or even a tertiary
order.[1]

The spiritual dimensions of what happened that Easter
Day may find expression also in a more outspoken wonder,
as in what Frederick Buechner has written in *The Magnificent Defeat:*

I cannot tell you . . . what I think I would have seen if I had
been there myself. . . . But I can tell you this: that what I believe
happened and what in faith and great joy I proclaim to you is
that he somehow *got up*, with the life in him again, and the glory
upon him. And I speak very plainly here, very unfancifully, even
though I do not understand well my own language. I was not
there to see it any more than I was awake to see the sunrise this
morning, but I affirm it as surely as I do that by God's grace the
sun did rise this morning because that is why the world is flooded
with light.[2]

Certainly a new light did shine and a new day begin when
his disciples said that they had seen the risen Jesus. They
themselves were changed, and the witnessing Christian
church was created—with a power which could make some
who had never before heard of Jesus exclaim: "Those who
have turned the world upside down have come here also"
(Acts 17:6). And Henrik Ibsen was only projecting in larger
terms the living power of the one who had been crucified
when he imagined the Roman Emperor Julian saying of
Jesus: "Where is he now? What if that at Golgotha, near

---

[1] P. G. S. Hopwood, *The Religious Experience of the Primitive Church*
(Edinburgh: T. and T. Clark, 1936), pp. 137-138.
[2] New York: Seabury Press, 1966, p. 80.

Jerusalem, was but a wayside matter, a thing done, as it were, in passing, in a leisure hour? What if he goes on and on, and suffers, and dies, again and again, from world to world?"[3]

So Jesus could not be got rid of by those who brought him to the cross. Neither could he be eclipsed by the passage of time.

It is true that much which is written and said in these latter days might seem to say that the sources of our knowledge are uncertain, and that a wide gulf divides the record of Jesus' life from our present understanding. "Form-criticism" and other analyses of the New Testament writings may appear to split the picture of him into fragments. But all the while the truth is that, for anyone who sits down to read the Gospels, a living awareness of what Jesus was like comes through. Geoffrey A. Studdert-Kennedy, that extraordinary Padre of the First World War, beloved by the common soldiers of the British Army and listened to by men of every rank, touched the essential reality when he wrote that even if the Gospel records are incomplete and the details not always clear, nevertheless—

There is One consistent Character which grows out of these pages until the student sees a Face and hears a Voice. It is so consistent that a thousand men can meet together and talk of Him, knowing that they have a common Friend, discovering again and again . . . that down widely different paths, and in all sorts of peculiar ways, the same Person has come to them out of the Gospel page. The critic may come in with his spectacles, scissors, and paste; he may take the Gospels to pieces and put them together again, but when he has finished the Voice still speaks, and the Eyes of Jesus still ask questions of the soul. The Character still stands. . . . Men have declared again and again that He was out of date, that He was dead and ought to be buried. Some have attacked Him scornfully, with bitter anger in

[3] *Emperor and Galilean* (New York: Charles Scribner's Sons, 1908), p. 456.

their eyes; some have forsaken Him sadly, with lingering regrets. But somehow He always appears to be the final Judge of His judges. . . . The pioneers of progress proclaim Him a reactionary, and then find themselves at a dead end with their reforms, because they need a "New Spirit" among the peoples; and it grows more evident every day that the New Spirit which they seek is as old as Jesus and as new. The critics contradict themselves, and cut one another out. Some say He is too joyful, some say He is too sad, some say He is too gentle, and some that He is too hard. To some He pipes and they will not dance, to others He mourns and they will not weep. But it all ends in this. With silent insistence the Character criticises the critics. If a man or woman or an age of men and women reject the Character, they do it at their peril, and time makes the peril plain. An age of luxury may reject His discipline, but time makes it clear that they are wrong. An age of materialism may reject His idealism, but their children will come seeking it again. An age of puritanism may condemn his gaiety and gentleness, but the pendulum will swing back again. An age of scientific knowledge may spurn his simplicity, but men come back with outstretched arms and empty hearts to ask the real questions that learning leaves unanswered for the soul.[4]

Also, it was not a traditionalist, but one of the "new theologians," who has written that even if our records have to be recognized as fragmentary, and no complete story of the life of Jesus can be recaptured, nevertheless "there is a great deal of material which gives us this history in the form of incidents, and enables us to catch glimpses of the man Jesus of Nazareth. . . . In each of them the figure at the center stands out boldly, even if we are unable to say just when and where the occurrence took place. From all these fragments, and from the way in which the early church responded to him, the originality and distinctiveness of the figure of Jesus of Nazareth may be seen."[5]

[4] *I Believe* (New York: George H. Doran Co., 1921), p. 75.
[5] Paul M. Van Buren, *The Secular Meaning of the Gospel* (London: S.C.M. Press, 1963), p. 120.

This "originality and distinctiveness" never meant some unearthly difference which would have made him aloof from the life of men about him. He was supremely what Dietrich Bonhoeffer called him, "the man for others." He had in him the qualities which men instinctively admire, which they may see in little flashes here and there in this person and that, but which were present in him with an intensity that made them like a flame. People in general were in bondage to their small timidities, but here was one who was master of himself, and had no fear of anyone. No dull conventions could cramp his thought, no threat from stubborn forces stand in the way of his self-forgetting purpose. When he followed his commitment to the Kingdom of God which he proclaimed, he treated the seeming barriers on his road as things to be scattered like so much straw. He had in him the opposite aspects which seldom go together: strength which made the powerful in the nation fear him, and yet the tenderness which made women and children, and all who were bewildered and troubled, turn to him. He could launch his terrible rebuke against the selfish and complacent, and go out with infinite compassion to the neglected and the lost. He could be what the self-righteous Pharisees scornfully called him, "the friend of publicans and sinners." Yet the compassion of Jesus toward imperfect human beings never was an indifferent indulgence which avoided a summons to their better selves. He gave new dignity to the man whose conscience had had no dignity, because he made him see himself in the light of God's expectation and recognize that what was reaching out to him to be redeeming must be relentless too.

That spirit of his can be seen and understood as it has been reflected in some of those who have learned from him—and in their learning shown the immortality of his influence. A little while ago there was a lovely person, wife and mother, and to many people outside her family a friend to whom they went instinctively because they knew that whatever troubled them she would understand. When she died, a young man whom she had deeply touched, wrote this of her.

I have been trying to sum up in my mind her many aspects. Perhaps the best description I can give of her is that she always had her feelers out making contact with humanity. She was extremely perceptive. This perceptivity would have been most disconcerting if she had not been so kind. Actually she was more than kind. She seemed to *feel* mankind. There was a broad understanding of our faults, but let any of us cross the line between what she accepted as human and what she condemned and you became very much aware of her moral values.

The fact that she was what she was came not by accident. Back of the happy human contacts there was an unseen comradeship, for her life was hid with Christ in God.

Thus it is true that the influence of Jesus, transmitted through the Gospel story, has brought, and can still bring, to sensitive human souls a sweetness and strength which are unmistakable. Just the awareness of what he was in the quality of his life, as one reads the Gospel story, warms the imagination and wakes something deep in the heart that makes men want to be better than they were before.

But the Christian belief in Jesus as the Savior has not come from the story of his life alone. It *is* an example, as set before the thought of men in Thomas a Kempis' classic *Imitation of Christ*. But no one could follow that example unless there were a power in it which rests upon a deeper fact. "*God* so loved the world that he gave his only Son," says the Gospel of John. Back of Jesus there was and is a transcendent Reality which is the source and strength of what men are meant to be.

To grasp and hold that saving truth it is necessary to separate conceptions which are changing and imperfect from what lies back of the words that have been used. Rudolf

Bultmann was right when he pointed out that some of the theological formulations which have been so long familiar have been bodied forth in terms which he calls mythical. That term "mythical" sounded at first startling and unwelcome, but in it there can be illumination. It does bring into light this which needs to be remembered: that spiritual experience and the living certainty of it cannot be transmitted in abstract phrases, and therefore will often be set forth in the pictures which for men of a particular time rise out of their instinctive thought. In the period of the New Testament and the early creeds, the forms and colors in which men's imaginative concepts were shaped—according to Bultmann—were inevitably these:

The world was viewed as a three-storied structure, with the earth in the centre, the heaven above and the underworld beneath. . . . the earth is the scene of the supernatural activity of God and his angels on the one hand, and of Satan and his daemons on the other. . . . "In the fulness of time" God sent forth his son, a pre-existent divine Being, who appears on earth as a man. He dies the death of a sinner on the cross and makes atonement for the sins of men. His resurrection marks the beginning of the cosmic catastrophe. Death, the consequence of Adam's sin, is abolished, and the daemonic forces are deprived of their power. The risen Christ is exalted to the right hand of God in heaven, and made "Lord" and "King." He will come again on the clouds of heaven to complete the work of redemption, and the resurrection and the judgment of men will follow. Sin, suffering and death will then be finally abolished. All this is to happen very soon; indeed, St. Paul thinks that he himself will live to see it.[6]

Such a picture of God and Christ and man, and such a conception of the drama of man's salvation, have actually been the orbit in which Christian thought has moved, down through the many centuries. It was John Milton, as we have

[6] *Kerygma and Myth,* edited by Hans Werner Bartsch (London: S.P.C.K., 1964), pp. 1, 2, 3.

seen, who put it into poetry; but innumerable believers, including Milton, have regarded it not only as poetry but as literal fact which could be set down also in dogmatic prose. Statements of faith which believers have been expected to sign, and forms of expression embodied in worship, have reflected—and still reflect—the picture of heaven and earth which men accepted in the years before Galileo and Copernicus. "O Lord, our heavenly Father, the high and mighty Ruler of the universe, who dost from thy throne behold all the dwellers upon earth. . . ."[7] "Christ did truly rise again from death, and took again his body, with flesh, bones, and all things appertaining to the perfection of Man's nature; wherewith he ascended into Heaven, and there sitteth, until he return to judge all Men at the last day."[8] "O Lord, Holy Father, Almighty, Everlasting God, for that thy dearly beloved Son Jesus Christ, for the forgiveness of our sins, did shed out of his most precious side both water and blood . . . sanctify this Water to the mystical washing away of sin."[9]

Expressions such as some of those are bound to seem unreal and meaningless to people of today—even to those who when they approach what has been hallowed by long tradition are altogether reverent. They know that there must always be new ways of interpreting truth; and it sounds today like an echo from some queer cave of obscurantism when one remembers that in 1894 the House of Bishops of the Protestant Episcopal Church declared that "fixedness of interpretation is of the essence of the creeds."

But meanwhile the matter of supreme importance is to discover whether there can be new ways of expressing truth without mutilating the truth itself. The danger in our time is that there has begun to be such mutilation. Some who have grown impatient with what they look upon as mythical de-

[7] The Order for Morning Prayer, Book of Common Prayer.
[8] Article IV, Articles of Religion.
[9] Office of Holy Baptism, Book of Common Prayer.

scriptions of the ways of God have come to the point of saying that we had better lay aside even the use of the word "God," since the old conceptions of what "God" was supposed to mean have no substance any more. So we have a chapter in *Honest to God* entitled "The End of Theism?" and from Van Buren a reflection of what he believes is a general opinion that "in a world 'come of age' . . . men no longer believe in a transcendent realm where their longings will be fulfilled."[10]

But that is a conclusion which the agelong instinct of our human race is never likely to accept. Those who have been touched at all by the faith which has focused in Jesus will go on looking for a way of understanding which leads through him to the Eternal One in whom he trusted and in whom we also can trust.

What may be some of the road marks on that way?

First is the realization that there is *something* in this universe besides the physical and the material. Somehow we human beings have been created; and created not as bodies only but as minds and spirits which reach out toward what is good and true and beautiful and can respond to values which are not seated in the flesh. The whole fact of being what we are makes us believe that everything significant that is in us—and much more—must be in whatever it was that created us in the beginning. If there are glimmerings of spirit in us, it must be that there was Spirit there.

Jesus of Nazareth brought into his world a quality of living which made the men who knew him feel a spiritual certainty which they had never had before. He walked in their familiar world, but he carried with him the atmosphere of another and mightier world from which he drew his strength. When he talked to them of God, what they listened to was no echo of an empty name. As they heard him, and as they watched him and went with him, they knew that he

[10] *The Secular Meaning of the Gospel,* p. 1.

was in contact with a source of power and grace that was
the fountain of his inner life. When they needed anything,
he reached out to them with a love that was bigger than
their deserving, and in which there was a lift that could not
be explained in any common way. They were not much on
speculation, but one thing they were sure of. Because of
what they saw in Jesus, God must be real; and God's reality
had come close to them.

*That* was the experience in which Christian faith began,
and that is the experience which shaped and reshapes theol-
ogies. When men of the early centuries tried to express the
*how* of this coming near of God, they did so in the concrete
spatial terms which to them made the experienced fact most
vivid. Jesus had brought a new dimension into life. Therefore he had come from another dimension. God was in
heaven, and Jesus had been there. Then he, the Son, had
come down to earth to share the lot of men, to take upon
himself the consequence of human sin, and by his life and
death to bring them back to God.

Put the same conviction now into a vaster frame, in which
our present thinking can find itself at home. Not at one particular moment only did the redeeming influence "come
down from heaven." From the beginning of time God who in
his holy purpose created us has sought to keep us in communion with his Spirit—or to bring us back into it when
self-will and sin had made us betray our heritage. Thus
through all human history the Creator would be the Re-
deemer also, and at the heart of God is the eternal Christ.
Whenever at any time and place there has been any human
soul in whom the holy love has been reflected, there has
been some foregleam of salvation. Then in the Man of Nazareth there was fashioned a mind and will so transparent
to the eternal purpose, and in his ministry of service so completely attuned to the infinite love, that in him the human
and the divine were made one.

Thus to feel that in Jesus the divine and human met is to say something that is not mythical, and not abstract. It is to express a faith that dares to interpret the unseen from the living wonder of the seen. The life of Jesus, and his consecration to the redeeming purpose that he followed even when its climax was the cross, moved always within the orbit of an infinite life and love that he felt to be encircling him—the life and love which he called "my Father and your Father." If that was so, then the dynamic which made Jesus what he was did not come first from the human side—as though the Man of Nazareth reached up toward the divine, until at length he touched it. Rather the initiative came from the eternal grace and power in which he lived and moved, and which was the coming near of God.

When Jesus was crucified, there was revealed the awful malignity of human sin. There is enough of the spirit in every man to make him recognize goodness when he sees it, but the challenge of goodness may be so intolerable to the rebellious will that men in their worst moments will go to any length to get rid of it. Then indeed they are under condemnation—not an angry condemnation visited upon them by what has been called "the wrath of God" but the awful condemnation *within* them of a guilty conscience which embitters the whole of life. From that condemnation the only deliverance can be when men recognize the love that has suffered for their sins, and yet reaches out, unwearied and unbroken, to become atonement. The profundity of meaning in the crucifixion is beyond the reaches of our thought, but in the deepest moments of our awareness *this* conviction irresistibly comes home: that on the cross there was not only one heroic man who would suffer to make men better, but an infinite purpose of redemption that is the reality of God. And Jesus, risen on Easter Day, stronger than evil and death, bringing new life not only to his first disciples but to numberless men and women since, is our witness that the God he trusted is the God in whom we can believe.

That being so, then hope and courage open out to great perspectives. Human souls that have tasted life most fully will not be persuaded that a "secular meaning of the Gospel" is enough: that we can get along without any transcendent Lord and work out our own salvation—or maybe find out that there is none. It might seem to have a brave sound if we should say that even if there is in the universe no eternal presence that is divine, we can each one be a "man for others," and that this will give life sufficient meaning. But there are hungers that will not be satisfied that way. Who, in the final reckoning, are we, and who are all "the others"? Little temporary centers of consciousness, flickering for a while like candle flames and presently to be blown out? And all the whole drama of human life, is that to go down at last into oblivion as though it had never been? Those whom we have loved and lost, the beautiful souls who gave to existence its precious central meaning, are they no more than disappearing memories? If it were so, then there would not be much but dust and ashes at the story's end. A prisoner escaped from that notorious penal settlement off the coast of French Guiana, "the Devil's Island," told of what it was about it that was most intolerable. Not the hard labor, not the climate, not the fever and the physical degradation, not even the brutality of human beings; but "the vast loneliness of the jungle and the sea, which shuts the prisoner off from the world into himself and drives him crazy."

Human life in general is no "Devil's Island." It is blessed with its great areas of beauty, and its intervals of joy. But it could become a place of desolation if at length it had to offer only a "vast loneliness of the jungle and the sea": the jungle of our ultimate bewilderments, and the empty sea of death beyond which there should be no divine horizon.

Sometimes in the poignant experiences of our human life there come to us intuitions of a life and a love that environ

us and are sufficient for all our need. In the second quarter
of this twentieth century, in Richmond, Virginia, there was
an orthopedic surgeon of great skill, Dr. William T. Graham.
But it was not his technical knowledge or the deftness of his
hands that made him best known and most regarded.
Rather, it was his compassion and his gentleness. Many people loved him, and especially all children did.

One day in the Crippled Children's Hospital there was a
small boy who was critically ill. An interne looking at him
told a nurse to watch him carefully, for he might not have
long to live. The doctor thought the child was asleep, but he
was not asleep, and he heard what the doctor said. Also,
suddenly, he remembered something else that he had heard.
Not long before, he had been in a church where a ranting so-
called evangelist had tried to frighten everybody into repentance, by cataloguing all the sins, real and imagined, for
which the unrepentant would be cast into hell. The child
thought he must be among the damned; and now he was
about to die—and he was terrified.

A minister who was in the hospital came and sat down by
his bed to try to comfort him. "God isn't that kind of a God,"
he said, "to want to deal harshly with a little boy even if—
like all the rest of us—he may have done something some
time that was wrong. God is not only greater than any of us,
he is more loving too. Could you think that I would let a
little boy go out alone into the darkness because he might
not always have been as good as he might have been?"

The child looked up at him, uncertain, and still troubled.
"I don't know, Mister," he said. "You see, I don't know you
very well."

For an instant the minister sat silenced, groping for the
word of assurance that would be real. He must find the right
thing to say and say it quick. Then it came to him.

"Do you know Dr. Graham?" he asked.

The child's eyes brightened. "Yes, everybody knows Dr. Graham."

"Do you think Dr. Graham could treat a little boy that way?"

"No," came the answer, "I don't think Dr. Graham would."

"Neither would God."

That night the child said to the nurse, "I'm not afraid any more, for God is like Dr. Graham."

Because of that beloved physician, the little boy had all he needed. If God whom he wondered about was like the man he knew, then everything must be all right.

What the child held to was the consequence of a greater fact; for the physician who meant so much to him was the kind of Christian who reflected the spirit of Jesus. That spirit and the power of it were expressed by the apostle Paul when he spoke in his Letter to the Romans of our human perplexities which can bring distress and tribulation, but in the midst of which stands not only the remembrance of Jesus but the power of his risen life. "In all these things," the apostle wrote in one great outburst of triumphant faith, "we are more than conquerors through him who loved us. For I am sure that neither death, nor life, nor angels, nor principalities, nor things present, nor things to come, nor powers, nor height, nor depth, nor anything in all creation, will be able to separate us from the love of God in Christ Jesus our Lord." The man through whom the little boy in the hospital was comforted had been the embodiment of that love, and through all the mystery of suffering he had been a witness to an eternal goodness that could be trusted, no matter what the look of things at any moment might seem to be.

So it is by contemplation of Jesus, and in what spoke through him of God, that we find the sustaining truth. Is there at the heart of the universe a Presence who can best be known by those who say "Our Father"? No arguments can prove that. No loud assertions could create a God who did not exist. But notwithstanding the questioning as to whether he is "up there" or "out there," there comes to men continually, as there came to Elijah in the wilderness, "a still, small voice" that says: He is here!

# VIII

## The Experienced Reality

WHERE do you find God?
In fullness of living, deep within, and wide without.

The trouble with many of us is that so much of whatever inner life we have is on the surface. The experiences of any ordinary day may be mostly a succession of distractions, to which we respond with little pieces of our attention and our energy. There is no controlling center of consciousness to keep us steady. But all the while there is a divine Reality that is waiting to come to the deeper self within us, and make us know that we are companioned by a Presence which is saying to us, "Be still, and know that I am God."

Phillips Brooks, who not only by what he said in the pulpit but by his whole great personality, made spiritual experience manifest as a living flame, described in one of his sermons the kind of human fact which by its analogy may make us aware of what the Presence of God can be. "You go into a room full of people," he said,

and the tumult of tongues is all about you. You are bewildered and distracted. . . . you feel lost. . . . In the presence of so many people, they all seem to take hold of you and claim some part of

99

you, whether they speak to you or not. You are lost in the crowd. You are merely part of the tumult. But by and by you meet your best friend there; somebody whose life is your life; somebody whom you sincerely love and trust; somebody who thoroughly satisfies you, and, by the contact of his nature, makes your taste and brain and heart and conscience work at their very best. As you draw near to him it seems as if you drew away from all the other people. As he takes hold of you, he seems to claim you and they let you go. The worry and vexation of the crowd sink away as he begins to talk with you, and you understand one another. By and by you have forgotten that all those other men are talking around you. You have escaped from the strife of tongues. You are absorbed in him. He has hid you in the secret of his presence.[1]

But does God actually come near in a way as understandable as that? it may be asked. Men possessed of some rare sensitiveness may have their clear and special consciousness of God. That can be granted. Again and again in religious history there have been those who seemed in some supreme moment to be lifted into another world; a St. Francis of Assisi, the mediaeval mystics, souls to whom there has come the beatific vision so that they appeared hardly to belong to this earth at all. Must we not recognize, though, that an awareness of God that will be significant comes only to the spiritually endowed, and not to the ordinary person in the ordinary place?

No. The truth is greater and more alive than that. Thomas R. Kelly, a man of our own century, who has written a modern classic concerning the inner life, *A Testament of Devotion*, was in his early years often restless and unhappy. Then, as his biographer was later to tell of him, "A new life direction took place. No one knows exactly what happened, but a strained period of his life was over. He moved toward adequacy. A fissure in him seemed to close, cliffs caved in and filled up a chasm, and what was divided grew together

[1] Phillips Brooks, *Sermons* (New York: E. P. Dutton, 1902), p. 83.

within him." And this is what one day he said to a group to whom he wanted to bring the certainty that he himself possessed:

To you in this room who are seekers, to you, young and old who have toiled all the night and caught nothing, but who want to launch out into the deeps and let down your nets for a draught, I want to speak as simply, as tenderly, as clearly as I can. For God *can* be found. There *is* a last rock for your souls, a resting place of absolute peace and joy and power and radiance and security. There is a Divine Center into which your life can slip, a new and absolute orientation in God, a Center where you live with Him and out of which you see all of life, . . . Eternity is at our hearts, pressing upon our time-torn lives, . . . calling us home unto Itself.[2]

What are some of the ways in which we ordinary folk, not accustomed to any mystical emotion, may yet have an actual sense of this "Eternity [which] is at our hearts, . . . calling us home unto Itself"?

It may come to us in some sudden response to the beauty of the world around us. A young artist, going out one breathless autumn morning along a wooded road where the gold and scarlet of New England maples lifted the palette of their incredible colors against the blue background of the hills, exclaimed, "I feel as though I just had to say 'Thank you' to somebody!" Some such feeling is likely to have come some time to nearly everyone. A poet, like Wordsworth or Shelley or Keats, could express the mystery and wonder of the beauty of the earth in words which the rest of us cannot command, but the fact is there for something deep within us all to register. To sit by the edge of a quiet lake as the shadows lengthen and the sounds of the day are hushed; to watch the sunset flame and fade, and to see the slow curtains of the darkness drawn, and then to gaze into the awesome depths beyond the kindling stars—is to know our little-

[2] New York: Harper & Row, 1941, pp. 18-19, 29.

ness, and yet in the same moment to feel encompassed by a sublimity which draws us toward itself.

A consciousness of that which is greater and more eternal than ourselves may come to us also whenever we recognize that which we *ought* to do. Why should there be such a thing as a sense of *oughtness?* Various humanistic explanations—or attempted explanations—may be given. Conscience may be represented as only the product of accumulated precedents and crowd pressure, so that we act in the way we happen to act only because we are pushed by social force in that direction. But when we are our fullest selves we know that the reality is more than that, and different. As John Baillie has written in *The Sense of the Presence of God*, "When I set myself to analyze my moral consciousness, I cannot doubt that it sets up to be a consciousness of standards that are not of my own making, of ends not of my own choosing, of commandments not of my own issuing. The whole dignity of man, the whole much boasted 'value of human personality,' resides in man's awareness of being thus under obligation to something greater than himself."[3]

When a man is faced by various possibilities of thought and conduct, what shall he ask himself about them, and on what basis shall he decide between them? Such and such a choice may be convenient, or profitable, or in line with general expectation. But there is an instinct in him that cannot avoid asking something else. What is *right?* And by what is right he means something which he cannot put exactly into words but which he feels compellingly: *a pull from up ahead.* An influence is reaching out to him which says, "This is the way; walk in it." He may not see all the length of the road, or even be able to tell himself explicitly *why* it is the right one, but he knows that a compass needle somewhere in his heart points in a sure direction: away from a mean or flabby contentment with what he already is; toward the integrity of motive, the courage, and the commitment to some

[3] New York: Charles Scribner's Sons, 1962, p. 31.

generous purpose which represents the larger person he may begin to be. And when he responds to this influence that leads him forward he has a new certainty and strength. He finds that he can face difficulties that formerly he would have flinched from, and carry on when before he would have stopped. The influence which has laid hold upon him is too steady, too penetrating—yes, and too relentless—to be impersonal. In the moments of his warm awareness he knows that it must be—God.

Again: a sense of dimensions in life which seem too great to mean anything less than God may come to us through the plain fact of human goodness. But what reason is there to draw any inference about God from that? it may be asked. What is so remarkable about goodness that a bland humanism cannot create? But is it as easy as that? The presence of social convention may keep men respectable, and make it not too difficult to be decent. But real goodness is something different from that. It has a fullness like the flooding of a fountain, as distinguished from the broken spurts that come from the labored action of a pump. It rises from artesian depths that lie hidden beneath the common ground. Rufus M. Jones, inspirer of the American Friends Service Committee, and one of the men of this century whose influence was most lifegiving, remembered how in his boyhood in a Quaker household "we never ate a meal which did not begin with a hush of thanksgiving; we never began a day without a family gathering at which Mother read a chapter of the Bible." And at the Quaker Meeting, "when occasionally the silence was broken by one or another speaking simply and quietly to God, he realized"—as his biographer was afterwards to write—"both the reason for the silence and the communion that was sought and experienced in it. Unconsciously he early acquired a conviction of the reality of the 'unseen world impinging on his world of things.' "[4]

[4] Elizabeth Gray Vining, *Friend of Life* (Philadelphia: J. B. Lippincott, 1958), p. 21.

People who have no special spiritual quality may have a brilliance of a kind. But now and then one sees a person through whom there seems to come a light that gives a more than earthly brightness to all the life they touch. Baron von Hügel was telling to a listener the four conditions which the Roman Catholic Church required to have been made manifest before anyone could be pronounced a saint: loyalty to the faith, heroism, endowment with powers beyond ordinary human capacities, and radiance. "They may possibly be wrong about those first three conditions," said von Hügel, "but they are gloriously right about that fourth commandment—a saint must be *radiant*."[5] Then when there *is* radiance, instead of the depressed and disillusioned look that so many faces wear, there must be a reason. And the reason is that a human soul, turning as the earth turns toward the sun, has looked toward One who in spiritual transcendence is "up there" and "out there," and so that soul has been illumined by a light that to the unconcerned might never have seemed to exist on land or sea.

But beyond all that has been said, there is the ultimate way by which the inner life finds God—or, rather, is found by God. It is through that which some may think of trivially or even vulgarly, but which every man whose life has not been tragically empty knows to have been the gift that has brought to him whatever largeness exists within his soul. Only four letters are needed to spell it, but all language cannot fully express what it may mean. For it is love.

The wistfulness, the longing, the pathos and the power of life—all are wrapped up in that word. When a man supposes that no one cares whether or not he even exists, like the convict passing through the railroad station, life can be a desert land. But one sign of an understanding human sympathy can be to him like an oasis in the sands. And not only for the man in acute need, but for every man, it is someone's

[5] Quoted in Vining, *op. cit.*, p. 205.

love that is the fountain which alone can give him the living water that keeps him on his feet. The remembrance of his mother (there is an old saying in the Talmud that God could not be everywhere and therefore he made mothers), or the trust of a little child, may save him when he is about to fall. And who can measure what can come to him through the woman who is his wife. Stupidity and blindness may destroy the meaning of marriage: but to some there has been given —and to all there is ready to be given—a discovery of the benediction that can come through a human love: in self-forgetfulness, in faithfulness, in the spirit that "bears all things, believes all things, hopes all things," and will never fail. Whoever has known that sort of spiritual comradeship will recognize that he has been enfolded in a reality not bounded by this earth; that "love is of God, and he who loves is born of God and knows God, for God is love."

"At the core of our personality is a spark lighted at the altar of God in heaven," wrote W. R. Inge, Dean of St. Paul's Cathedral, London, in his own *Confessio Fidei*, "an inner light which can illuminate our whole being." To maintain it, it is necessary "to purify the eyes of the understanding by constant discipline, to detach ourselves from hampering worldly or fleshly desires, to accustom ourselves to ascend in heart and mind to the Kingdom of the eternal values which are the thoughts and purposes of God."[6] Thus to know and to experience the reality of God there must be something more than absorption in secular concerns. There must be time for the secret contemplation and for the listening prayer in answer to which the Voice from beyond oneself may speak. In this sense, the full life can never be "religion-less." It recognizes that there must first be communion with the highest and holiest that we know before there can be some new and transforming light to shine on the roads of every day.

[6] *Outspoken Essays* (London: Longmans, Green & Co., 1923), p. 14.

So much, then, for the "deep within" which this chapter at its beginning spoke of. But fullness of living must be not only deep within, but "wide without." If what ought to be religion is not to stagnate into dead religiosity, he who would find the living God must look for him not in some supposed process for saving his own soul but in a response to human needs that lets him forget himself—and find his real self in that forgetting.

In an earlier chapter there was the kindling suggestion which came from a phrase of Anne Morrow Lindbergh, "Immersion in Life." She was expressing the exaltation of spirit which came to her when she went on a safari, without guns, into the midst of one of the great African preserves where the wild creatures still roam free, and watched and listened in "the stillness trembling with life like the stillness of a flame" until she felt herself so drawn into the circle of their immense existence that her own existence seemed enlarged. And the important fact is that there is an Immersion in Life on a higher plane which is open to every one of us, and can lift one out of self-involvement into contact with the Heart of Being—which is another name for God. That higher plane is human life; not human life in the abstract, but the lives of actual men and women with whom one becomes identified and learns anew the reality of God by what he sees in them. Strange unexpected things sometimes open windows of awareness into what the human heart may hold. When the Communists took possession of China, they ordered most Americans out. Alfred B. Starratt, then a missionary teacher at Hua Chung University, tells what happened to him when the police informed him that he must make his way down the Yangtse River to Shanghai for evacuation. Arriving at the riverbank, he was not allowed to board the regular ferry to Hankow, and was forced to bargain with the boatmen who rowed people across.

These men were wise enough not to take a foreigner accompanied by police to the other side without first demonstrating their "patriotism" by insulting one as a foreign dog and demanding impossible prices for the trip.

While this sport was being enjoyed by everyone except Er Lao [his household servant] and myself, another boatman came rowing down the river. He saw what was happening, heard the insults and derisive laughter. He swung his boat into the shore, jumped out and helped my friend Er Lao get my trunk aboard his boat without saying a word about the price of the trip. Before the others could recover from their astonishment, we had shoved off and were rowing toward Hankow. The police, who obviously had not liked this abrupt ending of the game any more than the other boatmen, rushed off to catch the motor ferry so that they could overtake us on the other side.

"This will bring you much grief, old one," I said to the man as he strained at his oar.

"It's not important," he replied, "I also am a man."

And when the Christian from America whom he had helped to rescue asked him about himself and what his religion was, he answered, "I don't know really what I am. But I know this—we both bleed the same color."[7]

Because each of us must say, "I also am a man" and "we bleed the same color," there is indeed a "secular meaning of the Gospel:" a secular meaning *not* in the sense that might be conveyed, of something "religionless," stripped of any transcendent reference: no, but secular nevertheless, on the great scale which recognizes the dignity of all ordinary life, and values it enough to want to bring to it an inspiration which comes from on high. We are creatures of this earth, and much of our existence is concerned with very mundane matters. But we do not have to be altogether earthy. In our human nature there are sparks of something glorious, as in the Chinese boatman; and the Christian gospel is the good news that these sparks *belong* there, for they are "the life of

[7] *The Real God* (Philadelphia: The Westminster Press, 1965), p. 12.

God in the soul of man." One of the great spiritual interpreters in this twentieth century helped all sorts of men and women to find new purpose in their common occupations and a new glow in all their living because he knew that the Spirit of God can "get at folks—ordinary, everyday folks—and that just as around our bodies there is a physical universe from which we draw all our physical energy, so around our spirits is a spiritual Presence in living communion with whom we can find sustaining strength."[8]

It is in identification with the "ordinary, everyday folks," and with the world they live in, that real Christianity must always find itself at home, and it is there that Christians will find God. When Wilfred Grenfell heard about the grim conditions among the deep-sea fishermen on the coasts of Newfoundland and Labrador and determined to go there and see what he could do, he said he wished that everybody could take a course in some university on what it really *means* "to love your neighbor." "Christ has become to me," he wrote, "to mean more and more *doing* something, anything, well. . . . Christ's religion to me is primarily for this world, and the new Jerusalem is to come down from Heaven onto this earth. . . . To every red-blooded man life becomes heaven in proportion as he seizes its opportunities for service." And the kind of service his religion impelled him to had exemplified already what Dietrich Bonhoeffer was afterward to reach for when he wrote that "To be a Christian does not mean to be religious in any particular way . . . but to be a man. It is not some religious act which makes a Christian what he is, but participation in the suffering of God in the life of the world,"[9] and in what might seem to the unimaginatively pious to be the very down-to-earth aspects of the world at that. "I can remember," Dr. Grenfell said,

[8] Harry Emerson Fosdick, *The Living of These Days* (New York: Harper & Row, 1956), pp. 78, 75.
[9] *Prisoner for God* (New York: The Macmillan Co., 1954), p. 166.

being blamed because my critics claimed that starting a lumber mill in order to give labour to hungry families, was not a rightful use for "mission" funds. When we accepted the gift of a site for a hospital on Caribou Island, Labrador, the deed stipulated that I must not sell pork or molasses, or . . . go into the grocery business. But the time came when it was apparent that that was exactly what Christ would do in that situation. Most of the necessities of life had to be imported in Labrador. The people lived on a truck or peonage system, and were paid in kind and not in cash. They did not know the value of the fish they caught or the price of the things they were buying. I remember being bitterly assailed for sending the "Trade Review" telling the prices of our produce and our necessities into different sections of the coast. When we actually . . . started a co-operative store four miles from a trader's station . . . we at once became anathema.[10]

Anathema or not, what he kept on doing in the name of Christ was to try "to subordinate my will to his," and to bring that will to bear upon the everyday conditions of human life where it was needed most.

Finding God in the midst of the world's work, and in what might be called the secular city, has been illuminated also in the career of another modern man. Dag Hammarskjöld, Secretary General of the United Nations, whose death in the mysterious destruction of an airplane in 1961 was a tragic loss to the whole world community which he served, had kept a diary which not even his close friends knew of, but which was found by his executor, together with a note allowing it be published, if that were so desired. As Hammarskjöld himself described it, it was "a sort of 'White Book' concerning my negotiations with myself—and with God."

There was a time when the words "with God" had not represented much to Hammarskjöld. In 1951, when he asked himself—as many a man may do—whether life has any ultimate significance, he wrote that even the question might be

[10] Wilfred Grenfell, *What Christ Means to Me* (Boston: Houghton, Mifflin Co., 1927), pp. 46, 40, 49.

absurd. "What I strive for is impossible, that my life should acquire a meaning. I dare not believe, I do not see how I shall ever be able to believe, that I am not alone." He did not say that "God is dead," but God had not then become for him inspiringly alive.

Not then; but the experiences of his life were to bring enlargement. The growth of his thought and the progress of his spiritual pilgrimage were revealed in an interview which Edward R. Murrow persuaded him to consent to when Hammarskjöld first came, in 1953, to his new and demanding responsibility at the United Nations. He called it *Old Creeds in a New World;* and this is part of what he said:

The world in which I grew up was dominated by principles and ideas of a time far from ours and, as it may seem, far removed from the problems facing a man of the middle of the Twentieth Century. However, my way has not meant a departure from those ideals. On the contrary, I have been led to an understanding of their validity also for our world today. Thus a never abandoned effort frankly and squarely to build up a personal belief in the light of experience and honest thinking has led me in a circle. I now recognize and endorse, unreservedly, those very beliefs which were once handed down to me.

From generations of soldiers and government officials on my father's side I inherited a belief that no life was more satisfactory than one of selfless service to your country—or humanity. . . .

From scholars and clergymen on my mother's side I inherited a belief that, in the very radical sense of the Gospels, all men were equals as children of God. . . .

"Faith is the union of God with the soul." . . . I was late in understanding what this meant. When I finally reached that point, the beliefs in which I was once brought up and which, in fact, had given my life direction even while my intellect still challenged their validity, were recognized by me as mine in their own right and by my free choice. I feel that I can endorse those convictions without any compromise with the demands of that intellectual honesty which is the very key to maturity of mind.

He went on then in that same interview and that *confessio fidei* to acknowledge the influence upon him of the attitude to life embodied in "the ideal of service" as Albert Schweitzer lived it, and "as set forth in the Gospels." And "the explanation of how man should live a life of active social service in full harmony with himself as a member of the community of spirit, I found in the writings of those great mediaeval mystics for whom 'self-surrender' had been the way of 'self-realization' and who in 'singleness of mind' and 'inwardness' had found strength."[11]

From the time when he entered upon his demanding work at the United Nations, his diary showed that increasingly he read and meditated upon the Bible and especially the Psalms and the Gospels, and upon one above all of the writings of the mediaeval mystics "who in 'singleness of mind' and 'inwardness' had found strength." Thomas à Kempis' *The Imitation of Christ* was the book which he took with him on what was to prove his fateful last flight to the Congo, and his copy of it was found on the bedside table of the room in which he had slept the night before he died. Meanwhile, there had come to him a certainty of purpose, and a sense of reinforcement in it, of which he had not known in earlier years. Looking back in 1961 (which, though he could not know it, was to be the last year of his life), he wrote on Whitsunday, "At some moment I did answer *Yes* to Someone —or Something—and from that hour I was certain that existence is meaningful and that, therefore, my life, in self-surrender, has a goal."[12] He had become possessed—as W. H. Auden has expressed it in his Foreword to the published *Markings*—by "the conviction that no man can do properly what he is called upon to do in this life unless he can forget

[11] Henry P. Van Dusen, *Dag Hammarskjöld* (New York: Harper & Row, 1967), p. 46.

[12] *Markings*, trans. W. H. Auden and Leif Sjöberg (New York: Alfred A. Knopf, Inc., 1964), p. 205. Used by permission of Alfred A. Knopf, Inc. and Faber and Faber Ltd.

his ego and act as an instrument of God."[13] And in 1961 Hammarskjöld had written this prayer:

> Give us
> A pure heart
> That we may see Thee,
> A humble heart
> That we may hear Thee,
> A heart of love
> That we may serve Thee,
> A heart of faith
> That we may live Thee.[14]

So it is not strange that the most recent interpreter of Hammarskjöld's life and spirit should have written concerning him.

In face of this man's pilgrimage, let no one—however steeped in the dominant relativisms, agnosticisms and negativisms of our day—let no one maintain that the ablest and most honest contemporary mind is unable to affirm informed and confident religious certitude.[15]

To find God in fullness of living, deep within and wide without: that was the thought with which this chapter began, and that may well be the double desire to hold to when all is said and done. Sometimes what the mediaeval mystics called the *vita contemplativa* and the *vita activa* have been spoken of as though they could be separated, and one group of men be "the religious" and the other "the secular." But that is to cut life in two, so that neither half reflects the greatness of God.

The contemplative life and the active life belong together.

In the noise and tumult of our modern times we deeply need to hear again the quiet words, "Be still, and know that I

---

[13] *Ibid.*, p. xvi.
[14] *Ibid.*, p. 214.
[15] Van Dusen, *op. cit.*, p. 212.

am God." There is sometimes a brash assurance which assumes that we know so much that we do not have to stop
and listen. But here the Quakers in their central experience
have much to teach us. There is an "Inner Light" which can
become visible to those—and only those—who are hushed
and waiting, as one waits for the stars to appear at the end of
day. The prayer that is most real is a listening prayer; and
one can believe that such were the prayers of Jesus when it
was recorded that he would go apart from the crowd and
even from his disciples to be alone with God. It was the
eternal Voice and not the voices of the world that he would
hear.

It is told of a great preacher in Scotland in an earlier
century that he had gone one day to a church where people
from near and far had thronged to listen to him. The hour
for service came, and he did not appear. As minutes went by,
the congregation grew perplexed; and one of the elders sent
the verger to the robing-room to find out what had happened. After a while the verger returned, to say that he had
knocked at the door without response, but that he had heard
the minister walking back and forth, absorbed—it seemed—
in conversation with someone who was there. He was saying
again and again, "I cannot go out, I will not go out, unless
You go with me." At length he did come out—and through
the open door the congregation saw only what appeared to
be an empty room, where no one else had been. Into the
pulpit, his face uplifted, the minister went; and it was recorded afterward that when he began to preach that day, "he
was singularly assisted."

But also it is true that one does not have to be alone to
hear the Voice of God. It is the listening and not the alone-
ness which matters most. Jesus joined in the worship of the
community where he was. He went into the synagogue on
the Sabbath day "as his custom was"—because there was the
expression of the corporate faith by which each single per-

son could be fortified. So the continuing worship of the Christian church has its everlasting value, and only the impatient and the shallow will forget it. There is the flame of a continuing witness to all that the many generations have believed and lived by—the flame from which may be lighted and relighted the little candles of single souls whose light when the winds blow strong may flicker and go out. Bishop Robinson, in *Honest to God,* has spoken refreshing truth when he has made bold to say that ecclesiastical emphasis on "devotional practices," and the kind of "prayer life" which is mainly withdrawal and retreat, can actually enfeeble and not set forward a virile commitment to the work of God. Yet over and above that warning stands the fact that no man can give what he does not have; and if any man is to bring a kindling spirit to the world he is a part of he had better have tried in thought and deliberate desire to come close enough in prayer to God for some burning coal from the heavenly altar to light a fire in him.

Then when the fire is lighted in his own religious consciousness, his business is not to stand where he is and warm himself, but to go out into the weekday world of work and shared experience to see whether God is there. God in the "sacred" surroundings, yes; but what about God in "the secular city"? To see what people may be up against, at home, on the streets, at the places where they make their living, is to be sure of this: that life can be a very drab and weary business when there is no quickening purpose and no sense of a horizon wider than the crowding facts. But then something else appears. Here is a woman in some shabby little house, nursing a sick child with an unflagging devotion and a tenderness that makes the tired eyes light up with beauty. Here is a man working against heavy odds to earn enough to feed his family, and trying his best not to show to those who depend on him the hopelessness to which sometimes he could almost yield. And here is another who in a close temptation keeps his moral integrity, and in whatever may be the test of loyalty to those who trust him will never let them down. Suppose that one who sees realities like these begins to let his sympathies enlarge, until he becomes so sensitive both to all the wistfulness and to all the wonderfulness that can be in human lives that he wants to bring the best that is in him to those who need what he might give. Then he has found the way in which life, and faith in the Giver of life, expand.

The supreme embodiment of union between the depths of life and the wideness of life was in Jesus. All the way from Galilee to Gethsemane, in the communion of his prayers he drew from the infinite depths of God; and the power that then belonged to him went out to meet the needs of the least and lowliest to whom his strength and compassion could minister. For individuals and for Christian congregations, that should be the ideal now.

When the Riverside Church had been planned and was being built in New York City, many people told themselves and said to one another "how wonderful" it would be when that magnificent structure should be finished and the congregation take possession of it. Then Harry Emerson Fosdick, its minister, answered:

It is not settled yet whether or not the new church will be wonderful. That depends on what we do with it. If we should gather a selfish company there, though the walls bulged every Sunday with congregations, that would not be wonderful. If we formed there a religious club, greatly enjoying themselves . . . that would not be wonderful.

But if all over the world, at home and abroad, wherever the Kingdom of God is hard bestead, the support of this church should be felt and, like an incoming tide, many an estuary of human need should feel its contribution flowing in, that would be wonderful. . . . If wherever soldiers of the common good are fighting for a more decent international life and a juster industry, they should feel behind them the support of this church which, though associated in the public thought with prosperity and power, has kept its conviction clear that a major part of Christianity is the application of the principles of Jesus to the social life, and that no industrial or international question is ever settled until it is settled Christianly, that would be wonderful. And if in this city, this glorious, wretched city, where so many live in houses that human beings ought not to live in, . . . where unemployment haunts families like the fear of hell, and two weeks in the country in the summertime is a paradise for a little child, if we could lift some burdens and lighten some dark spots and help to solve the problems of some communities, that would be wonderful. If in that new temple we simply sit together in heavenly places, that will not be wonderful; but if we also work together in unheavenly places, that will be.[16]

So, for life and what can be its fullness, there shines the truth which a contemporary Christian has expressed: "When I am concerned about myself, all wrapped up in myself, thinking only about myself, . . . I die. When I love, when I forget myself, when I lose myself, I live."[17]

It is in that kind of service that we find, and are found by, God.

[16] *The Living of These Days,* p. 194.
[17] Theodore P. Ferris, *What Jesus Did* (New York: Oxford University Press, 1963), p. 103.

248.483 Bo
Bowie, Walter Russell
Where you find God

DATE         ISSUED T

248.483 Bo
Bowie, Walter Russell
Where you find God